Hardscrabble

John Richardson

Contents

HARDSCRABBLE

BY

John Richardson

CHAPTER I.

It was on a beautiful day in the early part of the month of April, 1812, that four persons were met in a rude farm-house, situated on the Southern Branch of the Chicago river, and about four miles distant from the fort of that name. They had just risen from their humble mid-day meal, and three of them were now lingering near the fire-place, filled with blazing logs, which, at that early season, diffused a warmth by no means disagreeable, and gave an air of cheerfulness to the interior of the smoke-discolored building.

He who appeared to be master of the establishment was a tall, good looking man of about forty-five, who had, evidently, been long a denizen of the forest, for his bronzed countenance bore traces of care and toil, while his rugged, yet well-formed hands conveyed the impression of the unceasing war he had waged against the gigantic trees of this Western land. He was habited in a hunting-frock of grey homespun, reaching about half way down to his knee, and trimmed with a full fringe of a somewhat darker hue. His trowsers were of the same material, and both were girt around his loins by a common belt of black leather, fastened by a plain white buckle, into which was thrust a sheath of black leather also, containing a large knife peculiar to the backwoodsmen of that day. His feet were encased in moccasins, and on his head, covered with strong dark hair, was carelessly donned a slouched hat of common black felt, with several plaited folds of the sweet grass, of the adjoining prairie for a band. He was seemingly a man of strong muscular power, while his stern dark eye denoted firmness and daring.

The elder of the two men, to whom this individual stood, evidently, in the character of a superior, was a short thick-set person of about fifty, with huge whiskers that, originally black, had been slightly grizzled by time. His eyebrows were bushy and overhanging, and almost concealed the small, and twinkling eyes, which it required the beholder to encounter more than once before he could decide their true color to be a dark gray. A blanket coat that had once been white, but which the action of some half dozen winters had changed into a dirty yellow, enveloped his rather full form, around which it was confined by a coarse worsted sash of mingled blue and red, thickly studded with minute white beads. His trowsers, with broad seams, after the fashion of the Indian legging, were of a dark crimson, approaching to a brick-dust color, and on his feet he wore the stiff shoe-pack, which, with the bonnet bleu on his grizzled head, and the other parts of his dress already described, attested him to be what he was--a French Canadian. Close at his heels, and moving as he moved, or squatted on his haunches, gazing into the face of his master when stationary, was a large dog of the mongrel breed peculiar to the country--evidently with wolf blood in his veins.

His companion was of a different style of figure and costume. He was a thin, weak-looking man, of middle height, with a complexion that denoted his Saxon origin. Very thin brows, retrousse nose, and a light gray eye in which might be traced an expression half simple, half cunning, completed the picture of this personage, whose lank body was encased in an old American uniform of faded blue, so scanty in its proportions that the wrists of the wearer wholly exposed themselves beneath the short, narrow sleeves, while the skirts only "shadowed not concealed," that part of the body they had been originally intended to cover. A pair of blue pantaloons, perfectly in keeping, on the score of scantiness and age, with the coat, covered the attenuated lower limbs of the wearer, on whose head, moreover, was stuck a conical cap that had all the appearance of having been once a portion of the same uniform, and had only undergone change in the loss of its peak. A small black leather, narrow ridged stock was clasped around his thin, and scare-crow neck, and that so tightly that it was the wonder of his companions how strangulation had so long been avoided. A dirty, and very coarse linen shirt, showed itself partially between the bottom of the stock, and the uppermost button of the coat, which was carefully closed, while his feet were protected from the friction of the stiff, though nearly wornout, military shoes, by wisps of hay, that supplied the absence of the sock. This man was about five and thirty.

The last of the little party was a boy. He was a raw-boned lad of about fourteen years of age, and of fair complexion, with blue eyes, and an immense head of bushy hair, of the same hue, which seemed never to have known the use of the comb. His feet were naked, and his trowsers and shirt, the only articles of dress upon him at the moment, were of a homespun somewhat resembling in color the hunting frock of his master. A thick black leather strap was also around his loins--evidently part of an old bridle rein.

The two men first described, drew near the fire and lighted their pipes. The ex-militaire thrust a quid of tobacco into his cheek, and taking up a small piece of pine board that rested against the chimney corner, split a portion off this with his jack-knife, and commenced whittling. The boy busied himself in clearing the table, throwing occasionally scraps of bread and dried venison, which had constituted the chief portion of the meal, to the dog, which, however, contrary to custom, paid little attention to these marks of favor, but moved impatiently, at intervals, to the door, then returning, squatted himself again on his haunches, at a short distance from his master, and uttering a low sound betwixt a whine and a growl, looked piteously up into his face.

"Vat the devil is de matter wid you, Loup Garou?" remarked the Canadian at length, as, removing the pipe from his lips, he stretched his legs, and poised himself in his low wood-bottomed chair, putting forth his right hand at the same time to his canine follower. "You not eat, and you make noise as if you wish me to see one racoon in de tree."

"Loup Garou don't prate about coons I guess," drawled the man in the faded uniform, without, however, removing his eyes from the very interesting occupation in which he was engaged. "That dog I take it, Le Noir, means something else--something more than we human critters know. By gosh, boss," looking for the first time at him who stood in that position to the rest of the party--"If WE can't smell the varmint, I take it Loup Garou does."

At this early period of civilization, in these remote countries, there was little distinction of rank between the master and the man--the employer and the employed. Indeed the one was distinguished from the other only by the instructions given and received, in regard to certain services to be performed. They labored together--took their meals together--generally smoked together--drank together--conversed together, and if they did not absolutely sleep together, often reposed in the same room. There was, therefore, nothing extraordinary in the familiar tone in which the ci-devant soldier now addressed him whose hired help he was. The latter, however, was in an irritable mood, and he answered sharply.

"What have you got into your foolish head now, Ephraim Giles? You do nothing but prophesy evil. What varmint do you talk of, and what has Loup Garou to do with it? Speak, what do you mean?--if you mean anything at all."

As he uttered this half rebuke, he rose abruptly from his chair, shook the ashes from his pipe, and drew himself to his full height, with his back to the fire. There had been nothing very remarkable in the observation made by the man to whom he had addressed himself, but he was in a peculiar state of mind, that gave undue importance to every word, sounding, as it did, a vague presentiment of some coming evil, which the very singular manner of the dog had created, although he would scarcely acknowledge this to himself.

The man made no reply, but continued whittling, humming, at the same time, the air of "Yankee Doodle."

"Answer me, Ephraim Giles," peremptorily resumed his master; "leave off that eternal whittling of yours, if you can, and explain to me your meaning."

"Etarnal whittling! do you call it, Boss? I guess it's no such thing. No man knows better nor you, that, if I can whittle the smallest stick in creation, I can bring down the stoutest tree as well as ere a fellow in Michigan. Work is work--play is play. It's only the difference, I reckon, of the axe and the knife."

"Will you answer my question like a man, and not like a fool, as you are?" shouted the other, stooping, and extending his left hand, the fingers of which he insinuated into the stock already described, while, with a powerful jerk, he both brought the man to his feet, and the blood into his usually cadaverous cheek.

Ephraim Giles, half-throttled, and writhing with pain, made a movement as if he would have used the knife in a much less innocent manner than whittling, but the quick, stern eye of his master, detected the involuntary act, and his hand, suddenly relinquishing its hold of the collar, grasped the wrist of the soldier with such a vice-like pressure, that the fingers immediately opened, and the knife fell upon the hearth.

The violence of his own act, brought Mr. Heywood at once to a sense of the undue severity he had exercised towards his servant, and he immediately said, taking his hand:

"Ephraim Giles, forgive me, but it was not intended. Yet, I know not how it is, the few words you spoke just now made me anxious to know what you meant, and I could not repress my impatience to hear your explanation."

The soldier had never before remarked so much dignity of manner about his Boss, as he termed Mr. Heywood, and this fact, added to the recollection of the severe handling he had just met with, caused him to be a little more respectful in his address.

"Well, I reckon," he said, picking up his knife, and resuming his whittling, but in a less absorbed manner, "I meant no harm, but merely that Loup Garou can nose an Injin better than ere a one of us."

"Nose an Indian better than any one of us! Well, perhaps he can--he sees them every day, but what has that to do with his whining and growling just now?"

"Well, I'll tell you, Boss, what I mean, more plain-like. You know that patch of wood borderin' on the prairie, where you set me to cut, t'other day?"

"I do. What of that?"

"Well, then, this mornin' I was cuttin' down as big an oak as ever grew in Michigan, when, as it went thunderin' through the branches, with noise enough to scare every buffalo within a day's hunt, up started, not twenty yards from it's tip, ten or a dozen or so of Injins, all gruntin' like pigs, and looking as fierce as so many red devils. They didn't look quite pleasant, I calculate."

"Indeed," remarked Mr. Heywood, musingly; "a party of Pottawattamies I presume, from the Fort. We all know there is a large encampment of them in the neighborhood, but they are our friends."

"May-be so," continued Ephraim Giles, "but these varmint didn't look over friendly, and then I guess the Pottawattamies don't dress in war paint, 'cept when they dance for liquor."

"And are you quite sure these Indians were in their war paint?" asked his master, with an ill-concealed look of anxiety.

"No mistake about it," replied Giles, still whittling, "and I could almost swear, short as the squint was I got of 'em, that they were part of those who fought us on the Wabash, two years ago."

"How so, den, you are here, Gile. If dey wicked Injin, how you keep your funny little cap, an' your scalp under de cap?"

This question was asked by the Canadian, who had hitherto, while puffing his pipe, listened indifferently to the conversation, but whose attention had now become arrested, from the moment that his fellow-laborer had spoken of the savages, so strangely disturbed by him.

"Well, I don't exactly know about that, myself," returned the soldier, slightly raising his cap and scratching his crown, as if in recollection of some narrowly escaped danger. "I reckon, tho', when I see them slope up like a covey of red-legged pattridges, my heart was in my mouth, for I looked for nothin' else but that same operation: but I wur just as well pleased, when, after talkin' their gibberish, and makin' all sorts of signs among themselves, they made tracks towards the open prairie."

"And why did you not name this, the instant you got home?" somewhat sternly questioned Mr. Heywood.

"Where's the use of spilin' a good dinner?" returned the soldier. "It was all smokin' hot when I came in from choppin', and I thought it best for every man to tuck it in before I said a word about it. Besides, I reckon I don't know as they meant any harm, seein' as how they never carried off my top-knot;--only it was a little queer they were hid in that way in the woods, and looked so fierce when they first jumped up in their nasty paint."

"Who knows," remarked Mr. Heywood, taking down his rifle from the side of the hut opposite to the chimney, and examining the priming, "but these fellows may have tracked you back, and are even now, lurking near us. Ephraim Giles, you should have told me of this before."

"And so," replied the soldier, "I was goin' to, when Loup Garou began with his capers. Then it was I gave a parable like, about his scentin' the varmint better nor we human critters could."

"Ephraim Giles," said Mr. Heywood, sharply, while he fixed his dark eye upon him, as if he would have read his inmost soul, "you say that you have been a soldier, and fought with our army on the Wabash. Why did you leave the service?"

"Because," drawled the ex-militaire, with a leering expression of his eye, "my captin was a bad judge of good men when he had 'em, and reckoned I was shammin' when I fell down rale sick, and was left behind in a charge made on the Injins at Tippecanoe. I couldn't stand the abuse he gave me for this, and so I left him."

"Cool, indeed," sneered Mr. Heywood; "now then, Ephraim Giles, hear my opinion. Your captain thought you were a coward, for he judged you from your conduct. I, too, judge you from your conduct, and have no hesitation in pronouncing you to be a rogue or a fool."

"Well, I want to know!" was the only rejoinder of the man, as he went on unconcernedly with his whittling.

"Le Noir," said his master to the Canadian, who, imitating his example, had taken down a long duck gun from the same side of the hut, "take your dog with you and reconnoitre in the neighborhood. You speak Indian, and if any of these people are to be seen, ascertain who they are and why--"

Here he was interrupted by the gradually approaching sounds of rattling deer hoofs, so well known as composing one of the lower ornaments of the Indian wardress, while, at the same moment, the wild moaning of Loup Garou, then standing at the front door-way, was renewed even more plaintively than before.

Mr. Heywood's cheek blanched. It was not with fear, for he was a man incapable of fear in the common acceptation of the word, but independently of certain vague apprehensions for others, his mind had been in a great degree unhinged by an unaccountable presentiment of evil, which instinctively had come over it that day. It was this, that, inducing a certain irresoluteness of thought and action, had led him into a manifestation of peevish contradiction in his address to Ephraim Giles. There are moments, when, without knowing why, the nerves of the strongest--the purposes of the wisest, are unstrung--and when it requires all our tact and self-possession to conceal from others, the momentary weakness we almost blush to admit to ourselves.

But there was no time for reflection. The approach to the door was suddenly shaded, and in the next instant the dark forms of three or four savages, speedily followed by others, amounting in all to twelve, besides their chief, who was in the advance, crossed the threshold, and, without uttering a word, either of anger or salutation, squatted themselves upon the floor. They were stout, athletic warriors, the perfect symmetry of whose persons could not be concealed even by the hideous war-paint with which they were thickly streaked--inspiring anything but confidence in the honesty or friendliness of their intentions. The head of each was shaved and painted as well as his person, and only on the extreme crown had been left a tuft of hair, to which were attached feathers, and small bones, and other fantastic ornaments peculiar to their race--a few of them carried American rifles--the majority, the common gun periodically dealt out to the several tribes, as presents from the British Government, while all had in addition to their pipe-tomahawks the formidable and polished war-club.

Such visitors, and so armed, were not of a description to remove the apprehensions of the little party in the farm-house. Their very silence, added to their dark and threatening looks, created more than mere suspicion--a certainty of evil design--and deeply did Mr. Heywood deplore the folly of Ephraim Giles in failing to apprise him of his meeting with these people, at the earliest moment after his return. Had he done so, there might have been a chance, nay, every assurance of relief, for he knew that a party from the fort, consisting of a non-commissioned officer and six men, were even now fishing not more than two miles higher up the river. He was aware that the boy, Wilton, was an excellent runner, and that within an hour, at least, he could have reached and brought down that party, who, as was their wont, when absenting themselves on these fishing excursions, were provided with their arms. However, it might not yet be too late, and he determined to make the attempt. To call and speak to the boy aside, would, he was well aware, excite the suspicions of his unwelcome guests, while it was possible that, as they did not understand English, (so at least he took it for granted) a communication made to him boldly in their presence, would be construed into some domestic order.

"Wilton," he said calmly to the boy, who stood near the doorway with alarm visibly depicted on his countenance, and looking as if he would eagerly seize a favorable opportunity of escape, "make all haste to the fishing party, and tell Corporal Nixon who commands it, to lose no time in pulling down the stream. You will come back with them. Quick, lose not a moment."

Delighted at the order, the boy made no answer, but hatless--shoeless as he was, disappeared round the corner of the house. Strange to say, the Indians, although they had seemingly listened with attention to Mr. Heywood while issuing these directions, did not make the slightest movement to arrest the departure of the boy, or even to remark upon it--merely turning to their chief, who uttered a sharp and satisfied "ugh."

During all this time, Mr. Heywood and Le Noir stood at some little distance from the Indians, and nearly on the spot they had occupied at their entrance, the one holding his rifle, the other his duck-gun, the butts of both, resting on the floor. At each moment their anxiety increased, and it seemed an age before the succor they had sent for could arrive. How long, moreover, would these taciturn and forbidding-mannered savages wait before they gave some indication of overt hostility, and even if nothing were done prior to the arrival of the fishing party, would these latter be in sufficient force to awe them into a pacific departure? The Indians were twelve in number, exclusive of their chief, all fierce and determined. They, with the soldiers, nine; for neither Mr. Heywood nor Le Noir seemed disposed to count upon any efficient aid from Ephraim Giles, who, during this dumb scene, continued whittling before the Indians, apparently as cool and indifferent to their presence, as if he had conceived them to be the most peaceably disposed persons in the world. He had, however, listened attentively to the order given to Wilton by his master, and had not failed to remark that the Indians had not, in any way, attempted to impede his departure.

"What do you think of these people, Le Noir," at length asked Mr. Heywood, without, however removing his gaze from his visitors. "Can they be friendly Pottawattamies?"

"Friendly Pottawattamies! no, sare," returned the Canadian seriously, and shrugging up his shoulders. "Dey no dress, no paint like de Pottawattamie, and I not like der black look--no, sare, dey Winnebago."

He laid a strong emphasis on the last word, and as he expected, a general "ugh" among the party attested that he had correctly named their tribe.

While they were thus expressing their conjectures in regard to the character and intentions of their guests, and inwardly determining to sell their lives as dearly as possible if attacked. Ephraim Giles had risen from his seat in the corner of the chimney, and with his eyes fixed on the stick he was whittling, walked coolly out of the door, and sauntered down the pathway leading to the river. But if he had calculated on the same indifference to his actions that the Indians had manifested towards the boy, he was mistaken. They all watched him keenly as he slowly sauntered towards the water, and then, when he had got about half way, the chief suddenly springing to his feet, and brandishing his tomahawk demanded in broken, but perfectly intelligible English, where he was going.

"Well, I want to know," exclaimed the soldier, turning round, and in a tone indicating surprise that he had thus been questioned--"only goin over thar," he continued, pointing to the haystacks on the opposite side of the river, around which stood many cattle, "goin I guess to give out some grub to the beasts, and I'll he back in no time, to give you out some whisky." Then, resuming his course, he went on whittling as unconcernedly as before.

The chief turned to his followers, and a low, yet eager conversation ensued. Whether it was that the seeming indifference of the man, or his promise of the whisky on his return, or that some other motive influenced them, they contented themselves with keeping a vigilant watch upon his movements.

Mr. Heywood and the Frenchman exchanged looks of surprise; they could not account for the action of Ephraim Giles, for although it was his office to cross the river daily for the purpose he had named, it had never been at that period of the day. How the Indians could suffer his departure, if their intentions were really hostile, it was moreover impossible for them to comprehend; and in proportion as the hopes of the one were raised by this circumstance, so were those of the other depressed.

Mr. Heywood began to think that the suspicions of the Canadian were un- founded, and that their guests were, after all, but a party of warriors on their way to the Fort, either for purposes of traffic with the only merchant residing in its vicinity, or of business with the officer commanding. It was not likely, he reasoned, that men coming with hostile designs, would have suffered first the boy to be despatched on a mission which, obscurely as he had worded his directions, must in some measure have been understood by the chief; and, secondly, permitted Ephraim Giles to leave the house in the manner just seen--particularly when the suspicion entertained by him as well as by Le Noir and himself, must have been apparent.

But the Canadian drew no such inference from these facts. Although he could not speak the Winnebago language, he was too conversant with the customs of the Indians, to perceive, in what they permitted in this seeming confidence, anything but guile. He felt assured they had allowed the boy to depart on his errand SOLELY that they might have a greater number of victims in their power. Nothing was more easy, numerous as they were, than to despatch THEM, and then, lying in ambush among the trees that skirted the banks, to shoot down every one in the fishing boat before a landing could be effected, and preparations made for defence; while, in the indifference of their conduct in regard to the departure of Ephraim Giles, he saw but a design to disarm suspicion, and thus induce them to lay by their arms, the reports of which would necessarily alarm the party expected, and so far put them on their guard as to defeat their plans. The very appearance of Giles, moreover, crossing the water, if seen by the descending boat would, he thought they imagined, be a means of lulling the party into security, and thus rendering them a more easy prey.

While the master and the servant were thus indulging their opposite reflections, without, however, making any intercommunication of them, Ephraim Giles, who had now thrust his knife and stick into the pocket of his short skirt, shoved off the only canoe that was to be seen, and stepping into it, and seizing the paddle, urged it slowly, and without the slightest appearance of hurry, to the opposite bank, where, within less than ten minutes, he had again hauled it up. Then, as coolly ascending the bank, he approached one of the haystacks, and drew from it a few handfuls of fodder which he spread upon the ground, continuing to do so, as the cattle assembled around, until he had gained the outermost haystack bordering immediately upon the wood. This reached, he gave a loud yell, which was promptly answered by the Indians, who had continued to watch his movements up to the very moment of his disappearance; and darting along a narrow path which skirted the wood, ran with all his speed towards the Fort. His flight had not lasted five minutes, when the reports of several guns, fired from the direction he had just quitted, met his ear, and urged him to even greater exertion, until at length, haggard and breathless, he gained his destination, and made his way to the commanding officer, to whom he briefly detailed the startling occurrences he had witnessed.

CHAPTER II.

The Fort of Chicago, at that period, stood upon a portion of the same ground occupied by its successor, and was, in fact, a very epitome of a fortress. On the western side, two block-houses constituted its chief defence, while on the north, a subterranean passage led from the parade-ground to the river, near the banks of which it had been erected. The uses of this sally port were two-fold--firstly, to afford the garrison a supply of water in the event of a siege--secondly, to facilitate escape, if necessary. The country around, now the seat of fruitfulness and industry, was at that time a wilderness, tenanted only by the savage, and by the few daring and adventurous whites who had devoted their lives to purposes of traffic, yet whose numbers was so small as to induce them, with a view to their safety, to establish themselves as near the Fort as possible. Roads, there were none, and the half formed trail of the Indian furnished the only means of communication between this distant port, and the less thinly-settled portions of Michigan. Nor were these journeys of frequent occurrence, but performed at long intervals, by the enterprising and the robust men--who feared not to encounter privations and hardships--camping at night in the woods, or finding a less desirable repose in the squalid wigwam of the uncertain Indian.

The mouth of the Chicago River was then nearly half a mile more to the south-ward than it is now. At a short distance from the lake, which gives its name to the territory, it soon branched off abruptly to the north, and then again, taking another turn, pursued its original westernly coarse, and, passing near the Fort, gave to the latter the appearance of a slightly elevated peninsula, separated only from the water by a gentle declivity of no great extent. On the same side of the river was the Government Agency House, and at about a quarter of a mile from that, a spot generally used as a place of encampment by the friendly Indians--at that moment occupied by a numerous band of Pottawattamies. Immediately opposite to the Fort, stood the residence and trading establishment of Mr. Mackenzie--a gentleman who had long mixed with the Indians--had much influence with, and was highly regarded by them; and, close to his abode, lived with his family, consisting of his wife and her sister, French Canadians like himself, Ouilmette, one of the most attached of his people, and enjoying almost equal popularity with the red men. About a quarter of a mile beyond Ouilmettes, and immediately opposite to the Pottawattamie encampment, from which it was divided only by the river, was another small but neat dwelling. This belonged to Mr. Heywood, and was then inhabited by his wife and daughter, whom he would not permit to reside at the farm, as well on account of its rudeness of accommodation, as of the dread of exposing them, in that remote situation, to the very danger which we have seen he had himself so recently encountered.

Such was the civilian population of that sparsely inhabited country in 1812. Let us now see the strength of its garrison.

For the defence of so distant an outpost, almost cut off, as we have already shown, from communication with the more inhabited portions of the States, the American government had not thought it requisite to provide more than a single company of soldiers, a force utterly inadequate to contend in a case of emergency, with the hordes of savages that could be collected around them within a few hours, and WEEKS before any efficient succor could be obtained. This error, grave at any time, in those who sought to extend the influence of their name and arms throughout that fertile region which has now, within little more than a quarter of a century, become the very head of American commerce and navigation, was especially so at this particular epoch, when the Indian spirit, stirred to action by the great chief who had so recently measured his strength with his hated enemies at Tippecanoe, was likely to be aroused on all occasions where facility of conquest seemed to present itself. And, yet, that government well knew that there were, even at that moment, difficulties existing between themselves and Great Britain of a character to lead to an interruption of the friendly intercourse that had hitherto subsisted between the two countries, and which, if suffered to ripen into hostilities, would necessarily, associate many of the Indian tribes with the forces of England, drawing down certain destruction on those remoter posts, whose chief reliance on immunity from danger, lay, in a great degree, in the array of strength they could oppose to their subtle and calculating enemy.

This company, consisting, of seventy-five men--many of them married and with families--was under the command of an officer whose conduct throughout the eventful and trying scenes about to be recorded, has often been the subject of much censure--with what justice our readers must determine.

Captain Headley was one of those officers who, without having acquired no greater rank at the age of forty than he now possessed, had served in the army of the United States from his boyhood, and was, in all the minutiae of the service, a strict disciplinarian. He had, moreover, acquired habits of deference to authority, which caused him, on all necessary occasions, to regulate his conduct by the orders of his superiors, and so strongly was this engrafted on his nature, that while he possessed mind and energy sufficient to plan the most feasible measures himself, his dread of that responsibility which circumstances had now forced upon him, induced the utmost disinclination to depart from the letter of an instruction once received, and unrevoked.

These, however, were purely faults of his military education. To a commanding person and dignified manners, Captain Headley united a mind highly cultivated, and feelings and sentiments which could not fail to secure the respect even of those who were most ready to condemn that caution and prudence of character which so eminently distinguished his career as a subordinate soldier. It was well known and conceded that, if he erred, the error grew not so much out of his own want of judgment, but was rather the fruit of the too great deference to authority which led him, implicitly, to adopt the judgment of others. In the private relations of life, he was deservedly esteemed, excelling in all those higher accomplishments that ensure favor with society, and seldom fail to win for their possessor the approbation of women. Such, indeed, had been his success in this particular application of the gifts with which nature had endowed him, that he had, for some years, been the possessor of the affections and the hand of one of the noblest of her sex, whom, however, we shall take a later opportunity of introducing to the reader.

The next officer in rank was Lieutenant Elmsley, married also, and about ten years the junior of Headley. From causes, which will be explained in the coarse of our narrative, the subaltern did not incline to place that confidence in the measures and judgment of his captain, which, it has been shown, the latter almost invariably accorded to HIS superiors, and hence arose feelings, that, without absolutely alienating them--for, in their relative military positions this could never be--rendered their intercourse daily more and more formal, until, in the end, a sentiment almost of enmity prevailed. In a remote garrison like this such an evil was the more to be regretted, even while there was the greater probability, from absence of serious occupation, of its occurrence.

The junior subaltern was Ensign Ronayne, a high-spirited young Southerner, who had now been three years at the post, and within that period, had, by his frank demeanor, and handsome person, won the regard of all--military and civil--there and in the neighborhood. Enterprising, ardent, fearless, and chivalrous, this young man had passed the first year of what he, then, considered little short of banishment, in a restless desire for adventure; but at the end of that period, came a marked change over him, and the spirit that had panted exclusively for action, now bent before a gentler and a holier influence.

Last of the officers of this little fort, was the surgeon. Doctor Von Vottenberg, who as his name would imply, was a descendant from one of the earlier Dutch settlers in the colonies. There was nothing remarkable about this gentleman. He was short, stoat, rather of a bilious temperament--clever in his profession, and much addicted to compounding whisky punch, which he not only brewed, but drank most satisfactorily. What other attributes and accomplishments he possessed, the incidents herein related must develop.

It has been said that, on its Western side, the Fort was protected by two blockhouses, while on the northern a sally port communicated with the tower. On each side of the sally port were two small stores, reserved for the ammunition and arms, and for the provisions and spare clothing of the garrison. On the north and south faces, rose a series of small low wooden buildings, appropriated to the officers, and capable of containing thrice the number now occupying them. The southern face, or that which looks towards the locale of the scene described in our last chapter, was now the residence of the commanding officer, and of his senior subordinate, who, with their families and domestics, tenanted the whole of that range of buildings, with the exception of one large room in the centre, generally used as a hall of council with the Indians. In the other range, precisely similar in construction, were quartered Ensign Ronayne and the surgeon Von Vottenberg, who each, however occupied but one apartment. The central and largest serving as their mess-room. The other half of the building was vacant, or rather had been so, until the doctor obtained the permission of the commanding officer to use it as a temporary surgery--the hospital being a distinct edifice between the two block-houses. These latter, capacious for the size of the fort, accommodated the non-commissioned officers and men--the company being divided as equally as possible between the two.

Without the whole of these buildings stood a strong stockade, about twelve feet high, loop-holed for musquetry, with a bastion at each angle, facing the four principal points of the compass, on each of which was placed a small gun, that the men had been trained to work. The entrance to the fort was from the westward, and in the direction of the agency house, which two of these bastions immediately flanked.

The guard consisted of a non-commissioned officer and nine men--three sentries being furnished for the necessary duties--one for the stores already described--another for the commanding officer's quarters--the mess-room and the surgery, and the third for the, southern bastion, upon which floated the glorious stars and stripes of the Union. A fourth sentry at the gate had been dispensed with, in consequence of the proximity to it of the guard-house. This, was a small building immediately in front of the hospital, which, with the gate, came particularly under the surveillance of the non-commissioned officer of the guard.

With the character for strict attention to discipline, which has been ascribed to Captain Headley, it will be easily understood that every man on duty was expected to be as correct in the execution of its details, as though he had been at the Head Quarters of his regiment, or at the Seat of Government itself. The utmost regard to dress, and to the efficiency of arms was moreover enjoined, and so far did their commander feel indisposed to trust the inspection of them to the non-commissioned officer of the guard, that, although there were in the Fort, but two regimental officers besides himself, he had, from the moment of assuming the command, required them alternately to perform the necessary duties; superintending the relief of guards, and parading all men off duty and out of hospital, in full dress, at least once in the twenty-four hours.

At the outset, this had been a source of much discontent with the men, who conceiving that, in that remote region, the rigor of the service might be dispensed with, almost openly expressed their desire that there might be sent to command them, some officer less severe in his exactions. This had been reported to Captain Headley by his senior subaltern, from whose manner, while communicating the information, it was apparent that he did not wholly disapprove of a remonstrance against measures which involved the sacrifice of his own comfort. His superior was not slow to remark this, he, however, quietly observed that he was not, at his years, and in his responsible position, to be told the duty required to be performed by the troops under his command; and that, if he perceived any symptoms of insubordination, he would take the proper means to suppress it. The lieutenant made no reply, but bit his lip, and withdrew. This was the first manifestation of any thing approaching to disunion, between these two officers.

Lieutenant Elmsley, although by no means a negligent officer, was no disciplinarian. He could not but look upon formal guard mountings and parades, in that isolated quarter, as unnecessary--serving only to create discontent amongst the men, and to induce them--the unmarried especially--to desert, whenever an opportunity presented itself; while, bringing the subject more immediately home to himself, he deemed it to be a needlessly severe tax upon the only two subalterns of the garrison. This, he thought might, situated as they were, have been dispensed with, without the slightest inconvenience to the service; and the duty left to the superintendence of the non- commissioned part of the force. Hence his annoyance with his superior.

But Captain Headley was of a different opinion. He thought that the very remoteness of his post, rendered it the more necessary that no appearance of carelessness should be remarked by the tribes of Indians, who were in the vicinity, and who, however amicable their relations THEN with the United States, might later, from caprice or events yet unforeseen, take advantage of the slightest negligence, to attempt the destruction of all.

Better, he thought, that they who received the pay of the Government, for upholding its interests and dignity, should be subject to a frequent recurrence of duty--not in itself particularly irksome-than that an important post--the nucleus of the future prosperity of the State--should be perilled by the absence of that vigilance which ought to characterize the soldier. If he allowed to be retrenched, or indeed left unemployed, any of that military exhibition, which tends to impress upon the many the moral superiority of the few, where, he argued, would be their safety in the hour of need; and if those duties were performed in a slovenly manner, and without due regard to SCENIC effect, the result would be to induce the wily savage to undervalue that superiority which discipline chiefly secured to the white warrior. Captain Headley was discriminating and observant. He had, more than once, remarked the surprise and admiration created among the Indians who had access within the stockade, at the promptness and regularity of the system introduced into it, and this, of itself, was a sufficient motive to cause him to persevere in the course his judgment had adopted.

Such was the condition of affairs at the moment when Ephraim Giles, breathless with speed, and fancying the party of Winnebagoes close upon his heels, made his entry into the Fort. The news he brought was of a nature to assemble the officers, as well as many of the men and women, all anxious to hear the details of an occurrence, which now, for the first time since their arrival at the Fort, had created serious apprehension. But there was one of the party who manifested more than ordinary uneasiness. His impatience was great, and, after having whispered a few words in the ear of Captain Headley, and received an affirmative reply, coupled with an injunction of caution, he left the building in haste, and proceeded towards the block-houses, where, selecting half a dozen men, and ordering them to arm on the instant, he passed with them through the gate--sprang into a large scow which was unchained from its moorings, on the bank of the river, and pulled in the direction of the house already said to have been occupied by the wife and daughter of Mr. Heywood.

Meanwhile, Captain Headley closely interrogated the fugitive as to the number and appearance of the Indians who had created all this alarm, their probable object in visiting the farm in this seemingly hostile manner, and the number of shots he had heard fired. To all these questions the soldier, who had now, in some degree, recovered from his panic, replied in the usual drawling tone, his stick and knife, which had been drawn forth again from his pocket, in which he had deposited them in crossing from the farm-house, affording him his usual amusement, but nothing, of course, was elicited beyond what has already been related. Whether any one had been killed in the house, or the guns merely discharged to frighten the fugitive, or that the reports had proceeded from the fishing party that had been sent for, with a view to alarm the Indians, and deter them from the commission of outrage, were surmises that severally occurred to Captain Headley, but without enabling him to arrive at any definite opinion. That there was cause for apprehension, there was no doubt. The appearance of a band of strange Indians in the neighborhood, however small in number, dressed in their war-paint, gave earnest of coming trouble, not only through their own acts, but through the influence of example on the many other tribes whom they had been accustomed to look upon as friends and allies. In the midst of these reflections arose a feeling of self-gratulation that he had preserved that discipline and strict attention to duty, which, he knew, that all must now admit to have been correct, and which, if any difficulty did occur, could not fail to prove of the utmost importance.

His first consideration now was the safety of the small fishing party, to which allusion has more than once been made in the preceding pages, and which it was a source of satisfaction to him to recollect were, in accordance with an order never departed from on these and similar excursions, furnished with the necessary arms and ammunition, although only in their fatigue dress.

"Mr. Elmsley," he said turning to that officer, who stood waiting his orders, "who commands the fishing party?"

"Corporal Nixon, sir," replied the lieutenant, at once entering into his motive for the inquiry, "a brave, but discreet soldier, and one who, I am sure, will evince all necessary resolution, should he see anything of these Indians. The men who are with him are also fine young fellows, and among our best shots."

"I am glad to hear this," was the rejoinder, "but still, twelve Indians firing from the woods upon half their number in an open boat, and taken by surprise, would, I fear, render the activity, courage, and skill of these latter but of little avail. My hope is, that Corporal Nixon may see nothing of them, but that, on the contrary, if he has been apprised by the boy, as the fellow says he was to be, of their presence at Heywood's farm, he will make his way back without stopping, or at least, use every precaution to conceal himself, until he can drop down under cover of the darkness."

"What, sir," said the lieutenant, with a surprise he could ill conceal, "would you desire him not to afford the necessary succor to Mr. Heywood, if, indeed, he should be in time to render any service?"

"Mr. Elmsley," remarked his captain, somewhat sternly, "my sympathy for the fate of those at the farm, is, perhaps quite as strong as yours, but I have a higher stake at issue--a higher object than the indulgence of personal sympathy. I can ill afford, threatening as appearances are at this moment, to risk the lives of six men, the best you say in the fort, out of the very small force at my disposal. Nothing must be left undone to secure their safety. Order a gun to be fired immediately from the southern bastion. It will be distinctly heard by the party, and if not already apprised of the existing danger they will at once understand the signal. Moreover the report may have the effect of alarming the savages."

Lieutenant Elmsley withdrew to execute the order, and soon after the dull booming of a cannon was heard reverberating throughout the surrounding woods, and winding its echoes along the waters of the narrow and tranquil Chicago. So unusual an event as this excited a good deal of speculation, not only among the inmates of the Fort, but among the numerous friendly Indians encamped without, who, wholly unacquainted with the cause of the alarm, were, by the strict orders of Captain Headley, kept ignorant of the information of which Ephraim Giles had been the bearer--

That night there was a more than usual vigilance exercised by the sentinels, and although the rest of the garrison were exempt from extraordinary duty, the watchful and anxious commanding officer slept not until dawn.

CHAPTER III.

At a distance of about two miles above Heywood's farm, and on the southern branch of the Chicago, which winds its slightly serpentine course between the wood and the prairie. There was at the period of which we treat, a small deep bay formed by two adjacent and densely wooded points of land, in the cool shades of which the pike, the black bass, and the pickerel loved to lie in the heat of summer, and where, in early spring, though in less numbers, they were wont to congregate. This was the customary fishing spot of the garrison--six men and a non-commissioned officer, repairing there almost daily, with their ample store of lines and spears, as much, although not avowedly, for their own amusement, as for the supply of the officer's table. What remained, after a certain division among these, became the property of the captors, who, after appropriating to themselves what was necessary for their next day's meal, distributed the rest among the non-commissioned, and men of the company. As the season advanced, and the fish became more plenty, there was little limitation of quantity, for the freight, nightly brought home, and taken with the line and spear alone, was sufficient to afford every one abundance. In truth, even in the depth of winter, there was little privation endured by the garrison--the fat venison brought in and sold for the veriest trifle by the Indians--the luscious and ample prairie hen, chiefly shot by the officers, and the fish we have named, leaving no necessity for consumption of the salt food with which it was but indifferently stored.

On the day on which our narrative has commenced, the usual fishing party had ascended the river at an early hour, for the newness of the season and the shortness of the days rendered it an object that they should be on the accustomed haunt as soon as possible. They had left the Fort at daylight, passing Heywood's farm at the moment when, for the purpose of foddering the cattle on the opposite bank, he, with the boy Wilton, was crossing to the very canoe in which Ephraim Giles afterwards made his escape--the latter with the Canadian, being engaged in felling trees higher up the river.

Arrived at the little bay to which we have just adverted, the boat was fastened to the gnarled trunk of a tree, which projected over the deep water at the nearest point, and the party, taking with them their fishing rods, baits, and haversacks, but leaving their spears and muskets in the boat, dispersed themselves at short distances along the curve that formed the bay, which, however, was not more than three hundred yards in extent, from point to point.

When they first cast their lines into the water, the sun's rays were clearly visible through the thick wood in their rear. The early morning, too, had been cold--almost frosty--so much so, that the wild ducks, which generally evinced a good deal of shyness, NOW, seemingly emboldened by the briskness of the atmosphere, could be seen gliding about in considerable numbers, about half a mile below them; while the fish, on the contrary, as though dissatisfied with the temperature of their element, refused to do what the men called "the amiable," by approaching the hook. Their occupation had been continued until long past mid-day, during which time not more than a dozen fish had been taken. Vexed at his ill luck, for he had not had even a nibble, one of the men flung his rod upon the bank, impatiently, and then, seating himself on the projecting root of a large tree, declared it was all nonsense to play the fool any longer, and that the most sensible thing they could do, was to take their dinners--smoke their pipes--and wash the whole down with a little of the Monongahela.

"I say, Collins," remarked the corporal, good-naturedly, "we shall have poor fare for the officers' mess, let alone our own, if we all follow your example, and give up so soon. But, as you say, it's time to have some grub, and we'll try our luck afterwards."

"Rome wasn't built in a day," said the man who had been fishing next to Collins, and drawing in his line also, "we've a good many hours left yet."

Following the recommendation of the corporal, the rest of the party sat down on the edge of the bank, and, opening their haversacks, produced each his allowance of corn bread and venison, or salted pork, after dispatching which, with the aid of their clasp knives, they took a refreshing "horn" from the general canteen that Collins carried suspended over his shoulder, and then drew forth and lighted their pipes.

As the latter puffed away with a vigor that proved either a preoccupied mind, or extreme gratification with the weed, he cast his eyes carelessly down the stream, where a large description of duck, called by the French natives of the country, the cou rouge, from the color of their necks, were disporting themselves as though nothing in the shape of a fire arm was near them--now diving--now rising on their feet, and shaking their outstretched wings, now chasing each other in limited circles, and altogether so apparently emboldened by their immunity from interruption, as to come close to the bank, at a distance of little more than fifty yards from the spot where he sat.

"It's very ridiculous," he at length remarked, pouring forth at the same time, an unusual volume of smoke, and watching the curling eddies as they rose far above his head--"it's very ridiculous, I say, the captin's order that we sha'nt fire. Look at them ducks--how they seem to know all about it, too!"

"By gosh!" said another, "I've a good notion to fetch my musket, and have a slap into them. Shall I, corporal?"

"Certainly not, Green," was the answer. "If it was known in the Fort I had permitted any of the party to fire, I should be broke, if I did'nt get picketed for my pains, and none of us would ever get out again."

"No great harm in that, either," said the man who had made the novel observation that Rome had not been built in a day.

The corporal looked sharply at the last speaker, as if not fully comprehending his meaning.

"Jackson means no great harm if we never got out again," interposed Collins, "and I think as he does, for I see no fun in rowing four or five miles to fish, and scarcely getting a sight of one."

"Well, but Collins, that's not always our luck. I'm sure we've had sport enough before. It must be because the weather's rather cold today, that the fish won't bite."

"It's of no use his grumbling, Philips," remarked Corporal Nixon, "we're here, not so much for own sport as on a duty for the garrison. Let me hear no more of this, Collins."

"Well, corporal that's true enough," said Green, "but dash me if it isn't temptin' to see them fellows there stealin' upon us, and we lookin' on, and doin' nothin'."

"What fellows do you mean?" inquired the corporal, suddenly starting to his feet, and looking down the river.

"Why, them ducks to be sure, see how they come sailin' up to us, as if they knowed all about the captin's order--no jumpin' or friskin' now, but all of a heap like."

"Yes, but I say, what's that black looking thing beyond the ducks?" asked one who had not hitherto spoken, pointing his finger.

"Where, where, Weston?" exclaimed one or two voices, and the speakers looked in the direction indicated.

"Hang me if it isn't a bear," said Collins in a low, anxious tone; "that's the chap that has sent the ducks so near us. Do let me have a crack at him, corporal. He's large enough to supply us all with fresh meat for three days, and will make up for the bad fishing. Only one shy, corporal, and I engage not to miss him"

Sure enough, there was, in the centre of the stream, a dark object, nearly half a mile distant, which all joined in pronouncing to be a bear. It was swimming vigorously across to their aide of the river.

"I think we might take him as he lands," observed Green. "What say you, corporal; I reckon you'll let us try THAT, if you won't let us fire?"

"Stay all where you are," was the reply. "I can manage him myself with a spear, if I can only be in time before he reaches the shore. If not, it's no matter, for I won't allow a trigger to be pulled."

Corporal Nixon was a tall, active, strong-limbed Virginian. He soon cleared the space that separated them from the boat, and jumping to the stern, seized one of the fishing spears, and then moved on through: the wood that densely skirted the bank. But he had not been five minutes gone when he again made his appearance, not immediately by the half-formed path he had previously taken, but by a slight detour to the rear.

"Hist, hist," he said in an audible whisper, as soon as he saw that he was perceived, motioning at the same time with his hand to enjoin silence, and concealment. Then, beckoning to Weston to join him; he again moved along the path with the light tread of one who fears to alarm an object unconscious of interruption.

All had the sense to understand that there was some good reason for the caution of the corporal, and with the exception of Weston, who had promptly obeyed the signal, busily, but silently resumed their morning's occupation.

First, a quarter of an hour, and then minute after minute passed slowly away, yet there was no sign of the return of their companions. What could be the meaning of this? If the bear had not proved to be too much for them, they ought to have killed him, and rejoined them before this. Curiosity, nay, apprehension finally overcame the strong sense of obedience to orders, which had been literally drilled into them, and they all, at the suggestion of Green, dropped their rods on the bank, and moved cautiously in the direction that had been taken by the corporal and Weston. Great, however, was the surprise of Collins, then a little in advance, when, on nearing the spot where the boat lay moored, he beheld, not those of who they were in search, but a naked, and hideously painted savage, in the very act of untying the rope by which the skiff was fastened to the knotted and projecting root of the tree. Sensible that there was impending danger, although he knew not of what precise kind, inasmuch as there was no Reason to apprehend anything hostile from the Indians, with--all of whom around the fort, they had always been on friendly terms, he sprang forward to arrest the movement. But the distance was several rods, and the savage, alarmed by the rustling made among the foliage and brushwood in his rear, now put his shoulder to the boat, and, in the next instant would have had it far across this stream, had not a hand suddenly protruded from beneath the hollow clump of earth on which the tree grew, grasped him firmly by the ankle, even while in the act of springing into the forcibly impelled skiff. In a moment or two, he grappled tightly with his hands upon the bow of the boat, but, finding the pressure on his imprisoned limb too great for resistance, he relinquished his hold, falling upon his face in the water, from which he was dragged, although without violence, by Corporal Nixon, who had emerged from his hiding-place.

When the Indian was suffered to rise, there was a threatening expression on his countenance, which, not even the number of those by whom he was now surrounded could check, and he made an involuntary motion of his hand to his scalping knife, the only weapon with which he was armed, that lay in the sheath dangling from his girdle. Seeing, however, that there was no hostile disposition manifested by the party, he speedily relinquished his first impulse, and stood upright before them with a bold, but calm look.

"What you want with boat?" asked the corporal, almost involuntarily, and without the slightest expectation that his question would be understood.

"Me want 'em cross," replied the Indian, pointing to the opposite woods.

"But why you come in bear skin?" and, in his turn, the corporal pointed with his finger in the direction in which the supposed bear had been seen.

"Ugh!" grunted the savage doggedly, finding that he had been detected in his disguise.

"What nation you?--Pottawattamie?"

"Wah! Pottawattamie!"

"Curious enough," pursued the corporal, addressing himself to his comrades. "I don't half like the look of the fellow, but I suppose it's all right. We musn't offend him. You chief?", he continued, pointing to a large silver medal suspended over the breast of the athletic and well-proportioned Indian.

"Yes, me chief. Pottawattamie chief," and he made a sign in the direction of the Fort, near which the encampment of that tribe lay.

"You friend, then?" remarked the corporal, extending his hand.

"Yes, me friend," he answered promptly, brightening up and taking the proffered hand; "you give 'em boat?"

"Do you see any thing green in my eye?" asked the Virginian, incapable, even under the circumstances, of repressing the indulgence of his humor.

But the party questioned, although speaking a little English, was not sufficiently initiated in its elegancies to comprehend this; so, he merely answered with a "ugh!" while the greater portion of the men laughed boisterously, both at the wit of the corporal, and at the seeming astonishment it excited.

This mirth by no means suited the humor of the Indian. He felt that it was directed towards himself, and again he stood fierce, and with a dilating frame before them.

Corporal Nixon at once became sensible of his error. To affront one of the friendly chiefs would, he knew, not only compromise the interests of the garrison, but incur the severe displeasure of the commanding officer, who had always enjoined the most scrupulous abstinence from any thing offensive to them.

"I only meant to say," he added, as he again extended his hand. "I can't give 'em boat. White chief" and he pointed in the direction of the Fort, "no let me."

"Ugh!" exclaimed the Indian, his stern features again brightening up with a last hope. "'Spose come with Injin?"

For a moment or two, the corporal hesitated whether or not to put the man across, but when he reflected on the singular manner of his advent, and other circumstances connected with his appearance among them, his customary prudence came to his aid, and while avoiding all ground for offence by his mode of refusal, he gave him peremptorily to understand that there was an order against his suffering the boat to leave its present station.

Again the countenance of the Indian fell, even while his quick eye rolled incessantly from one to the other of the group. "You no give 'em boat--Injin swim," he at length observed.

"Just as you please," answered corporal Nixon. "By and bye, sogers go to the Fort--take Injin with 'em."

"Wah! Injin cross here," and as he spoke, he sprang again to the bow of the boat, and at a single bound cleared the intervening space to the very stern.

Several heavy splashes in the water.--a muttered curse from the corporal--some confusion among his men, and the savage was seen nearly half-way across the river, swimming like an eel to the opposite shore.

"Damn the awkward brute!" exclaimed the former, angrily. "How many muskets are there overboard, Jackson?"

"Only three--and two cartouch boxes."

"ONLY three indeed! I wish the fellow had been at old Nick, instead of coming here to create all this confusion. Is the water deep at the stern?"

"Nearly a fathom I reckon," was the reply.

"Then, my lads, you must look out for other fish to-day. Jackson, can you see the muskets at the bottom?"

"Not a sign of them, corporal," answered the man, as lying flat on the boat, he peered intently into the water. "The bottom is covered with weeds, and I can just see the tails of two large pikes wriggling among them. By Gemini, I think if I had my rod here, I could take them both!"

"Never mind them," resumed the corporal, again delivering himself of a little wit; "muskets will be of far more use to us just now than pikes. We must fish them up--there will be the devil to pay if we go home without them."

"Then there's no other way than diving for them," said Jackson, still looking downwards. "Not even the glitter of a barrel can I see. They must have buried themselves in the weeds. I say, Weston," slightly raising his head and turning his face to the party named, "You're a good diver?"

"Yes, and Collins is better than me."

"Well then, here's at it," resumed Jackson, rising and commencing to strip. "It's only by groping and feeling that we can find the arms, and when once we've tumbled on 'em, it will be easy enough to get 'em up with one hand, while we swim with the other. We must plunge here from the stern," he added, as the men whom he had named jumped on board and commenced stripping themselves.

"How came the Injin to knock the muskets overboard, Corporal?" inquired one of the party who had not yet spoken--a fat, portly man, with a long hooked nose, and a peaked chin.

"I'm dashed," replied Nixon, "if I can tell myself, though I was looking at him as he jumped from one end of the boat to the other. All I know is, the firelocks were propped against the stern of the boat as we placed them, with the backs of the cartouch boxes slung under the ramrods, and I suppose, for I don't know how else it could be done, that instead of alighting on the seat, he must have passed it, and putting his foot on the muzzles, tipped them with the weight of his body, head over heels into the water."

"Corporal," Ventured Collins, as he removed his last garment, "you asked that painted chap if he saw anything green in your eye. Now, that's as it may be, but hang me, if it wasn't a little green to take him for a Pottawattamie?"

"And how do you know he was'nt a Pottawattamie? Who made you a judge of Indian flesh?" retorted the corporal, with an air of dissatisfaction.

"Didn't he say he was, and didn't he wear a chiefs medal?"

"Say? Yes, I'll be bound he'd say and wear anything to gull us, but I'm sure he's no Pottawattamie. I never seen a Pottawattamie of that build. They are tall, thin, skinny, bony fellows--while this chap was square, stoat, broad-shouldered, and full of muscle."

Corporal Nixon pondered a little, because half-convinced, but would not acknowledge that he could have been mistaken. "Are you all ready?" he at length inquired, anxious, like most men, when driven into a corner on one topic, to introduce another.

"All ready," answered Jackson, taking the first plunge in the direction in which he knew the muskets must have fallen.

Before following his example, the others waited for his report. This was soon made. He had got hold of one of the muskets, and partly lifted it from its bed, but the net-work of strong weeds above it, opposing too much resistance, he had been compelled to quit his hold, and came to the surface of the water for air.

"Here's for another trial," shouted Collins, as he made his plunge in the same direction. In a few seconds he too, reappeared, bearing in his right hand, not a fire-lock, but the two missing cartouch boxes.

"Better luck next time," remarked corporal Nixon. "I think my lads, if two of you were to separate the weeds with your hands, so as to clear each musket, the other might easily bring it up."

The suggestion of the corporal was at once acted upon, but it was not, until after repeated attempts had been made to liberate the arms, from their Web-like canopy, that two were finally brought up and placed in the boat. The third they groped for in vain, until at length, the men, dispirited and tired, declared it was utterly useless to prosecute the search, and that the other musket must be given up as lost.

This, however, did not suit the views of the correct corporal. He said, pointedly, that he would almost as soon return without his head as without his arms, and that the day having been thus far spent without the accomplishment of the object for which they were there, he was determined to devote the remainder to the search. Not being a bad diver himself, although he had not hitherto deemed it necessary to add his exertions to those of his comrades, he now stripped, desiring those who had preceded him to throw on their shirts and rest themselves for another plunge, when he should have succeeded in finding out where the missing musket had lodged.

"What's that?" exclaimed Jackson, pointing to a small, dark object, of a nearly circular shape, which was floating about half way between the surface of the place into which the divers had plunged, and the weeds below.

His companions turned their eyes in the direction indicated, but, almost immediately after Jackson had spoken, it had disappeared wholly from view.

"What did it loot like?" asked the corporal.

"It must have been a mush rat," returned Jackson, "there's plenty of them about here, and I reckon our diving has disturbed the nest."

Corporal Nixon now took his leap, but some paces farther out from the shore than his companions had ventured upon theirs. The direction was the right one. Extending his arms as he reached a space entirely free from weeds, his right hand encountered the cold barrel of the musket, but as he sought to glide it along, in order that he might grasp the butt, and thus drag it endwise up, his hand disturbed some hairy substance which rested upon the weapon causing it to float slightly upwards, until it came in contact with his naked breast. Now, the corporal was a fearless soldier whose nerves were not easily shaken, but the idea of a nasty mush rat, as they termed it, touching his person in this manner, produced in him unconquerable disgust, even while it gave him the desperate energy to clutch the object with a nervous grasp, and without regard to the chance of being bitten in the act, by the small, sharp teeth of the animal. His consternation was even greater when, on enclosing it within his rough palm, he felt the whole to collapse, as though it had been a heavy air-filled bladder, burst by the compression of his fingers. A new feeling-a new chain of ideas now took possession of him, and leaving the musket where it was, he rose near the spot from which he first started, and still clutching his hairy and undesirable prize, threw it from him towards the boat, into the bottom of which it fell, after grazing the cheek of Collins.

"Pooh! pooh! pooh," spluttered the latter, moving as if the action was necessary to disembarrass him of the unsightly object no longer there.

A new source of curiosity was now created, not only among the swimmers, but the idlers who were smoking their pipes and looking carelessly on. All now, without venturing to touch the loathsome looking thing, gathered around it endeavoring to ascertain really what it was. "What do you make of the creature?" asked corporal Nixon, who, now ascending the side of the boat, observed how much the interest of his men had been excited.

"I'm sure I can't say," answered Jackson. "It looks for all the world like a rat, only the hair is so long. Dead enough though, for it does not budge an inch."

"Let's see what it is," said the man with the long hooked nose, and the peaked chin. By no means anxious, however, to touch it with his hands, he took up the spear and turned over and over the clammy and motionless mass.

"Just as I thought," exclaimed the corporal, with a shudder, as the weapon unfolding the whole to view, disclosed alternately the moistened hair and thick and bloody skin of a human head.

"Gemini," cried Jackson, how came this scalp here, it has been freshly taken--this very day--yet how could it get here?"

"Depend upon't," said Green, "that chief that was here just now, could tell somethin' about it, if he had a mind."

"Then he must have had it in his breech-cloth," remarked the corporal seriously, for not a rag besides had he about him. "No, no it couldn't be him, and yet it's very strange."

"Of course it couldn't be him," maliciously interfered Collins, who had so far conquered his first disgust, as to take the object of discussion into his own hands, "for you know he was a Pottawattamie, and therefore wouldn't scalp for the world."

"But whose can it be?" resumed Jackson, and how did it get here, I am sure its that of a boy."

"Could it have floated here from the farm?" half questioned Green musingly.

"Somethin' struck me like shots from that quarter, about an hour before the Injin swam across, and dash me, now I recollect it, I'm sure I heard a cry, just after the corporal left us to go after that bear."

"Nonsense," said the Virginian, "how could it float against the stream, and as for the shots you think you heard, you most have taken Ephraim Giles's axe blows for them. Besides, you couldn't hear shots at that distance. If you did, it most be from some of the hunters."

"But the cry, corporal," urged Jackson, "what say you to the cry Green says he heard when you left us?"

"All stuff; did anybody else hear it besides Green, you were all sitting on the bank with him?"

No one answering in the affirmative, Corporal Nixon declared the thing to be impossible, or he should have heard it too; nor could he see what connection there was between that cry--supposing there had been one--and the facts that had come immediately under their own observation.

"Hist," interrupted Collins, placing one hand upon the speaker's shoulder, and with the other directing his attention to what, now seen by the whole of the party, was ill calculated to re-assure them.

CHAPTER IV.

Stealthily gliding through the fresh and thinly foliaged wood, that skirted the opposite shore, yet almost concealed from view, Corporal Nixon now beheld the crouching forms of several armed Indians, nearly naked, and evidently in war costume. They were following the serpentine course necessitated by the interposing trees, and seeking cautiously to establish themselves behind cover on the very verge of the bank.

"Back men for your lives, there's nothing friendly there," exclaimed the Virginian the moment that his glance had taken in the scene, "out with the arms, and divide the dry ammunition. Collins, you are a smart fellow, do you and Green set to work and light a fire, but out of sight, and dry the muskets as fast as you can. There are twelve pounds in each of the five remaining cartouch boxes, these will do for a spell. Jackson, Philips, tree yourselves, while Cass lies flat in the stern, and keeps a good look out on the devils, without exposing himself. Now, my lads, do all this very quietly, and as if you didn't think there was danger at hand. If they see any signs of fear, they will pitch it into you directly. As it is, they are only waiting to settle themselves, and do it at their leisure."

"Pity they don't make a general of you, corporal," remarked Collins, as he proceeded quietly with Green to the execution of the duty assigned to them. "I guess Washington himself couldn't better command a little army. Is your battle order finished, general?"

"None of your nonsense, master Collins, this is no time for jesting. Go and dry these arms, and when you have them so that they can send a bullet from their throats, join Jackson and Philips in covering the boat. Weston and I will take up our first station."

And in less time than we have taken to describe the cause of the alarm, and the instructions given in consequence, the men had hastened to execute the several duties assigned to them on shore, while Cass remained, not only with a view of showing the Indians that the boat was not wholly unguarded, but to be enabled to inform his comrades, who could distinctly hear him without rendering any particular elevation of the voice necessary, of any important movement on the part of the former. This quietude of arrangement on the part of Corporal Nixon had, seemingly, been not without effect. It was evident that the Indians had no suspicion that they had been seen, and even when the men coolly quitted the boat, they showed no impatience indicative of an impression that the party were seeking to shield themselves from an impending danger.

"This silence is strange enough," said the corporal to his companion, after they had been some minutes secreted in the cavity from which the departure of the Indian with the boat had been arrested. "I almost wish they would fire a shot, for that would at once tell us how to act, and what we are to expect, whether they are friendly Indians or not."

But no shot was fired, and from the moment when the men quitted the boat, and took up their positions, everything had continued silent as the grave on the opposite shore, and not the vestige of an Indian could be seen.

"But for that scalp," again remarked the corporal, "I should take the party to have been friendly Indians, perhaps just returned from a buffalo hunt, and come down to the water to drink. They are surely gone again."

"Look there," said Weston, in a subdued tone, while he placed his hand on the shoulder of his superior, as both lay crouched in their hiding-place, "look there, corporal," and he pointed with his finger to the opposite bank. "Do you see that large, blackish log lying near the hickory, and with its end towards us?"

"I do--what of it?"

"Well, don't you see something crouching like between the log and the tree--something close up to both. See! it moves now a little."

Corporal Nixon strained his gaze in the direction indicated, but was obliged to admit that, although he distinctly enough saw the log and the tree, he could not discern any between thing them.

"NOW, do you see it?" again eagerly inquired Weston, as, at that moment, the same animal was seen to turn itself within the very limited space which had been indicated.

"Yes, I see it now," replied the Virginian, "but it's as likely to be a hog as a man, for anything I can make of that shape; a hog that has been filling his skin with hickory nuts, and is but now waking out of his sleep. Still, as the Injins were there just now, it may be that if they're gone, they've left a spy behind them. We'll soon know how matters stand, for it won't do to remain here all night. Cass," addressing the man in the boat who was seated low in the stern, only occasionally taking a sly peep, and immediately withdrawing his head, "place your cap on the rudder, and lie flat in the bottom. If they are there, and mean to fire at all, they will try their hands at THAT."

"I hope they are good marksmen, corporal," replied the man, as raising his right arm, he removed his forage cap and placed it so that the upper half only could be seen. "I've no great fancy for those rifle bullets, and give them a wide berth when I can."

"Now are you convinced?" asked Weston, addressing the corporal, as both distinctly saw the object upon which their attention had been anxiously fixed, raise his head and shoulders, while he deliberately rested his rifle against the log on his right.

"Close down, Cass--don't move," enjoined the Virginian; "the bait has taken, and we shall have a shot presently."

Two almost imperceptible jets of spiral smoke, and crack, crack, went two rifles, while simultaneously with the report, fell back into the boat, the perforated forage cap. Both balls had passed through it, and lodged in the heart of the tree to which the skiff was moored, and behind which Jackson and Philips had taken their stand.

Evidently believing that they had killed a man, the whole of the band, hitherto concealed behind logs and trees, now rose to their feet, and uttered a fierce and triumphant yell.

"Devilish good firin', that," remarked Green, whose face had been touched by a splinter of bark torn from the tree by one of the balls.

"Don't uncover yourselves, my lads," hastily commanded the corporal; "all the fellows want now is to see us exposed, that they may have a crack at us."

"We've dried the muskets after a fashion," said Collins, as he now approached Jackson and Philips. "Give us a cartridge, and let's see if we can't match the varmint at that sort of work." Then, having loaded, he, without asking the corporal's permission, leaned his musket against the tree, and taking a steady aim at the man who had fired from the point first noticed by Weston, drew the trigger.

The shot had evidently taken effect, for two other Indians were now seen going to the assistance of their comrade, whom they raised from the ground (where all had secreted themselves after the yell), and hurried to the rear.

A loud cheer burst from the lips of Collins, which was answered immediately by the whole of the savages, who, from various contiguous points, sprang again to their feet, and vociferating the war-whoop, dashed into the river nearly up to their necks, seemingly thirsting to overcome the only obstacle which prevented them from getting at their desired victims.

But, at the very moment, when several of them were holding their rifles aloft with their right hand, securing their powder-horns between their teeth, while Corporal Nixon issued to his men injunctions, not to pull another trigger until the savages should begin to swim, to the astonishment of all, came the sullen and unusual booming of the cannon from the Fort.

For a moment, the men, taking their eyes off the sights of their muskets, listened attentively for a repetition of the shot, but no second report reached their ears.

"That," said Green, "was a warnin' for us."

"It was," observed the corporal. "Had the danger been THERE, they would have fired again. Depend upon it, my lads, there's more going on about here than we think. So don't throw away your ammunition. Every bullet you send must tell!"

"Well, we can but sell our scalps as dearly as possible," interposed Collins, who had again loaded, and was now in the act of raising and supporting his, musket against the tree. "But look--see how the fellows are stealing off?"

"Don't fire, then, don't fire," hastily enjoined the corporal. "If they will go quietly, let them. We must not lose our time dallying here, but make our way back to the Fort. That gun was meant to recall us, as well as to warn us, and luckily it has frightened the Indians, so they won't care to attack us again."

Meanwhile the band of Winnebagoes, obeying, as it seemed, the command of their leader, whom Collins swore he could identify from his figure, even at that distance, to be the man who had attempted to carry off the boat, quitted the river for the cover of the woods, and, after an earnest consultation, retreated slowly in the direction of the prairie, without clamor of any description.

"Well rid of them, if they are gone," exclaimed the corporal, not a little relieved by their departure. "We must keep a sharp look out though, and see if they return."

"How many of them are there?" asked Jackson; "can you give a guess, Collins?"

"About a dozen I should say--indeed I counted as many as they passed through the small patch of clearing made by Eph. Giles's axe."

"Can they have started for the farm?" observed the corporal musingly; "if so, my lads, we had better get away as soon as possible, for there they will find canoes to cross."

"Why, sure they can swim across well enough. The river is not so wide as to prevent them from doing it on a pinch," remarked Philips.

"Of course they can," answered Collins, "but not without having their rifles as well soaked as our muskets were a little while ago. I say, corporal, I understand now the trick of that cunning chief. He jumped upon the arms purposely to overturn them into the river, when he found he couldn't get the boat, and all our firelocks over with him."

"Yes, that WAS a trick," remarked Jackson, "but, corporal, you havn't told us how the dickens that fellow came there, instead of the bear you went to spear."

"There is no time to talk about it, seriously rejoined the Virginian. Some night when we are on guard, I will tell you what little I know. At present let us see to getting back to our post. Collins, you are the crack shot of the party, are you loaded?"

"I am, corporal," returned the man somewhat self- sufficiently, "have you got another Injin for me to sink. If so, just point him out, and if this good barrel of Uncle Sam's don't do his job in no time, I'll give up all claim to having hit the first fellow."

"Not just yet," answered his superior, "but hear my orders. You'll follow the path along the bank, and move along carefully, until you reach Heywood's stacks. Conceal yourself behind one of them, until we come down with the boat, and keep a sharp lookout on all that you see passing in and round the farm. Now remember, Collins, not a shot, unless it be to save your life, or else you will get us all into a scrape."

"Never fear me, General Nixon, and he touched his cap with all the respect he would have accorded to an officer of that rank. I brought one of the imps down, and that, I reckon, is nearly as good work for one day, as filling the old boat with fish, or having a slap at them ducks, as I wanted this morning. But now I'm off, if I see anything shall I halloo out, and let you know there's danger?"

"Not by a long chalk," returned the corporal. "All I want you to do is to keep your tongue in your head and your eyes open. If you see anything to alarm you, come back quietly and let us know. We shall be moving down close to the bank of the river; and now start."

Collins threw his musket to the trail, and advanced cautiously, though fearlessly, along the scarcely perceptible pathway--interrupted, at every third or fourth step by creeping vines that protruded from the earth, and rendered it necessary, in order to prevent his tripping, that he should raise his feet somewhat in the manner of a horse with the string-halt.

He had not proceeded half a mile, when, at an angle of the ill-defined path, formed by a point where the river was the narrowest, he was started at the sight of a human body lying across his course, evidently on its face, though the head was concealed from view by the trunk of a large tree that bordered upon the road. His first impulse was to turn back and acquaint the corporal with what he had discovered; but a few minutes of reflection satisfying him of the ridicule he should incur in reporting, without being able to state with accuracy on WHAT, he boldly advanced. On approaching it, he found that the body was lifeless, while from the red and scalpless head, previously hidden from his view, were exuding gouts of thick blood that trickled slowly over the pale features of a youth of tender age, the expression of which had been worked up into an intensity of terror, and there remained. At a few paces from the head, and close upon the edge of the bank, lay a dressed bear skin which had evidently been saturated with water, but was now fast drying in the air and what little sunlight was occasionally thrown upon it, through the dense branches of the forest.

There are situations in which the mind is moved to do that from which in cooler moments it would shrink with disgust. It chanced that Collins had retained the scalp so singularly found at the bottom of the river, by Corporal Nixon, and this circumstance at once determined him.

Instead of hastening by an object so appalling, Collins rested his musket against a tree, and taking the scalp from between the ramrod and the stock, where he had introduced it, knelt by the body, and spreading out the humid skin to its fullest extent, applied it to the bleeding excavation. As he had suspected, they corresponded exactly, making all due allowance for the time they had been separated, and he had no longer a doubt that the mutilated boy was Mr. Heywood's help, Wilton. A much more important discovery than this, however, resulted from his vain endeavor to recognise the boy from his features, they were so contracted by terror, as has already been said, and so covered with blood as to be indistinguishable. But on turning him upon his back, and passing his hands over his face, Collins was surprised to find that there was not that icy chill which he had expected, but on the contrary the faint warmth that indicates suspended, animation; and deeper yet was the gratification of the rude soldier, when, on opening the shirt and placing his hand on the heart of the boy, he felt an occasional spasmodic pulsation, denoting that life was not utterly extinct.

With an eagerness to preserve life, strongly in contrast with his recent exultation in destroying it, his anxiety for the recovery of the boy was almost paternal. Fortunately the latter part of the day had been free from the chilliness of the morning, so that, although the naked skull must have been some hours exposed, the comparatively bland state of the atmosphere gave fair earnest that the brain itself, even if affected, had not sustained a mortal injury. Spreading wide the scalp in his open palm, Collins now breathed heavily upon it, until it attained what he conceived to be the necessary warmth, when gently applying it to the denuded crown, to which be fitted it as well as he could, he passed his handkerchief, which he had removed from his throat, over it, and under the chin of the boy in such a manner as to prevent the chill of the approaching night from affecting the injured part. This done, he poured through his closed lips a few drops of whisky from the canteen, and then raising him gently on his left shoulder, he rose from his stooping posture, and seizing in his right hand his musket, which he continued at the trail, pursued his route to the haystacks as directed.

In the meantime, Corporal Nixon, with the remainder of the fishing party, was slowly descending the river, hugging the eastern shore as closely as possible, in order that, if attacked suddenly, they might, on the instant, leap into the river, and covering themselves by the boat, fight their enemies at less disadvantage. The corporal himself and Weston kept a vigilant look out, the one at the bow, the other at the stern, while the four remaining men, Jackson, Philips, Green, and Cass pulled so noiselessly that the dip of their oars, and their unavoidable jar in the row-locks, could not be heard at a distance of more than ten yards. At this slow rate much time was necessarily consumed, so that it was quite dark when they reached the traverse opposite the farm, where Ephraim Giles had crossed some hours before, and whither Collins had been dispatched to make observations.

The patience of the latter had been much tried, for it seemed an age had elapsed before his comrades made their appearance. The sun was just setting as he reached the innermost haystack, and his anxiety for his charge had become intense. Seeing the canoe drawn up on the beach, and the paddles in it, he had a strong inclination to cross and procure some efficient relief for the insensible boy, but the silence that reigned around the dwelling awed him, and he checked the natural impulse. Not a soul was to be seen, not a voice to be heard, not even the barking of Loup Garou, the bleating of a sheep, or the lowing of an ox. What could this mean? and was the fate of the boy connected with that of the other inmates of the farm? If so, where were they?

Another consideration induced Collins to suppress his first impulse, and that was the apprehension that his strange charge would be detained by Mr. Heywood, when his only chance of recovery lay in the speedy examination, and dressing his injuries by the surgeon of the garrison. There was no alternative then, but to wait patiently for the arrival of the boat into which the boy could be placed; and so conveyed to the fort. Meanwhile, as the night air was becoming chill, and a slight fog rising from the water, the considerate soldier did all he could to shield his protege from their pernicious effect. Strewing on the ground a few armfuls of hay, taken from the nearest of the stacks, around which the hungry cattle now gathered, eager for their food, he extended on it the yet inanimate form of the youth, embracing the body in order to impart to it the benefit of animal heat and in this position, his head being slightly raised, eagerly endeavored to discern through the darkness not only what might be seen on the opposite shore, but the approach of the party in the boat.

The sun had now been down some time, and so dark was it that, in that narrow space, obscured by the blending shadows of the tall forests on either shore, it was difficult, at five yards distance, to make out anything on the water, unaccompanied by light or sound. This silence was anything but agreeable to Collins, whose imagination, excited by the later occurrences of the day, was filled with, strange misgivings, as he looked in vain for the customary lights in the farm-house. The fishing party had never been out so late, and yet, at the first fall of darkness, they had been accustomed to see the place exhibiting at least one light; and the absence of this now caused Collins heartily to wish himself in the boat, and safely moored under cover of the fort. Not that the soldier was influenced by the apprehension of personal danger, but because the deep gloom, the solitude and silence of the scene, coupled with his newly-awakened interest in the almost corpse that lay in close contact with his person, impressed him with a sort of superstitious feeling, not at all lessened by the knowledge that his only companion, at that moment, belonged rather to the grave than to the upper earth.

At length his anxiety was relieved. The sound of the oars, cautiously pulled, faintly met his ear, and then the boat could be indistinctly seen approaching the canoe. To this succeeded a low call uttered by the corporal. Collins replied in a similar tone, and then bearing the body of the boy, still enveloped in the bear skin, he in less than a minute, rejoined his party.

The astonishment of the latter may be conceived on beholding so unexpected a sight, nor was their feeling of awe diminished when their comrade had briefly related what had occurred since he left them.

"Strange enough, this," remarked the corporal musingly; "stranger still, there's no light in the house. It's neither too early nor too late for that. I'll tell you what, my lads, if any thing has happened we must know the worst--it will never do to go back to the Fort, without being able to give some notion of what took place under our very noses."

"What would Mr. Ronayne say, if we did?" added Jackson.

"Yes! and what would that sweet young lady, Miss Heywood, think of us, if we returned without giving some good news of her father. Why she never would look upon us kindly again."

"Right, Philips," said Weston, "and I'm sure I'd rather offend the captain himself, any day, than do anything to displease her. God grant we bring her no bad news."

"Amen," said the corporal, gravely, for he, like Collins, had some strong misgivings, arising naturally from the utter darkness and silence that continued to prevail in and around the farm-house. "Are you all loaded? Look to your primings, but make no noise. Somebody must take charge of the beat though. Who volunteers to remain, while the rest follow me to the house?"

"I do--I'll remain," said Collins, "one of you can take my musket"

"What, Collins, do you shirk the thing," sneered the man with the long nose and the peaked chin; "have you had enough to-day, or do you fear the ghost of the fellow you knocked over?"

"I fear neither man or ghost, as you well know, Nutcrackers," warmly rejoined Collins, "but I take it, there's no great courage in making a fuss about going where there's no enemy to be found. If there has been danger in that quarter, I take it, it's passed, and as somebody must stop in the boat, why 'not me as well as another?"

"Just so," said the corporal. "Cass, this is no time to run your rigs. You see well enough that Collins wishes to stop behind, on account of the boy he hopes to bring to life. Little chance of that, I fear, but if he thinks so, it would be unchristian to disappoint him. And now push off, but make no noise."

The order was obeyed. In a few minutes the bow of the boat touched the landing-place, when all but Collins, who was at the helm, slipped noiselessly ashore. The corporal repeated his instructions--how to act under emergency and if separated--and moved along the path leading to the house. Meanwhile Collins pulled back into the stream, and remained stationary in the centre.

CHAPTER V.

The farm-house was, as we have said, of very rude construction--such a one as could only spring up in so remote a region, and among so sparse a population. With the exception of the roof, the frame-work of which had been covered with raw buffalo hides, it was built wholly of rough logs, notched at the ends in a sort of dove-tail fashion, and when not lying closely, filled in with chunks of wood, over which a rude plaster of mud had been thrown, so that the whole was rendered almost impervious to water, while it ran little risk from the agency of fire. It had two rooms on the ground floor--one smaller than the other, used as a dormitory, and containing all the clothes or "traps," as they designated them, of the household. The other served as eating-room, parlor, and kitchen, and extended over, at least, three-fourths of the area. It was provided with two doors-- one facing the river and close to the partition which divided the rooms--the other occupying a remoter position to the rear. The windows of this apartment were two in number, and, equidistant from the doors, were considerably elevated above the floor. These apertures had been formed by simply sawing a few of the logs, so as to complete squares, into which were fitted rude sashes, each containing four small panes of a greenish, and by no means, transparent glass, and connected by strong leathern hinges. In winter the necessary warmth was afforded, by shutters put up and barred from within. The southern gable or dormitory, was provided in the centre with one window of similar size and construction. The upper floor, a sort of granary and depot for the provisions of the family, was ascended by means of a ladder, and through a square aperture just large enough to admit with ease the body of a man.

There was, in rear of the house, a rather extensive corn-field, and beyond the northern gable, where the chimney stood, an orchard yet in its infancy, but promising future abundance, while at the opposite, or south end of the building, a large but very highly cultivated garden, was now undergoing the customary spring process of digging and manuring, and indeed on that very morning, Mr. Heywood had been busily engaged in this occupation with the boy Wilton, his men being employed, the one in field labor, the other as we have seen, in chopping wood.

In the rear of the garden, and opposite to the corn-field, from which it was separated by a road leading to the wood, was a tolerably sized barn, likewise constructed of rude logs, not, however, filled in. The lower part of this was used as a stable; the upper or loft, roofed with bark, contained the preceding year's unhusked crop from the corn-field, while contiguous to it, and to the rear, was another oblong square building, constructed in the same manner, but without loft. This, partitioned and covered simply with unhewn logs, served not only as a pen for sheep and pigs, but as a roasting-place for the feathered portion of the stock.

The orchard on the one side, and the garden on the other, extended to the bank of the river--a zig-zag, or snake-fence separating them from the road, in the centre of which, and at about ten feet from the door of the dwelling, rose a majestic walnut tree then in early blossom. Immediately beyond this tree, was a low enclosure which intersected the road, passing across from the kitchen-garden to the orchard, and forming the only court or yard upon the premises.

When Corporal Nixon, with his little party, had cautiously advanced some few paces towards the house, he caused them to separate, Cass and Jackson leaping the fence which bounded the orchard, and Green and Philips that of the garden, while he himself, with Weston, pursued the pathway in front. The better to be prepared for any sudden attack, bayonets had been quietly fixed, and the firelocks at the full cock, carried at the trail--this latter precaution after the detached files had crossed the fences.

The night, as has already been said, was very dark, and each succeeding minute seemed to increase the obscurity, so that it was rather from their familiarity with the ground, than from any clear indication of correctness of course, that the little band were enabled to preserve their necessary unity. At length the tall shadows of the walnut tree came suddenly upon the sight of the corporal, but so completely absorbing was the darkness in the heavier gloom, that, without being aware of it's proximity, he stumbled against the low and slight enclosure, which, yielding to the impetus of his motion, feeble even as that was, caused him to fall forward on his face, his musket dropping from his grasp without, however, going off.

A low growl from a dog succeeded, and before the Virginian could even make the attempt to rise, the animal had sprang upon, and fastened his teeth into his shoulder, shaking him so violently, that it was not until Weston, who had now crossed the enclosure, came up to his assistance, guided by the sound of the struggle, that the dog could be made to relinquish his hold.

"Loup Garou--Loup Garou, old fellow, what's the matter with you," said the latter coaxingly, as he caressed the neck of the dog, which he had identified, and now sought to appease.

Evidently recognising a friend in the utterer of his name, the animal turned suddenly around, licked the hand of Weston, and then sent forth a long and piteous howl.

"Mercy, what is that?" suddenly exclaimed the corporal, who having regained his legs and musket, had moved on a pace or two.

"Where! what?" asked Weston, coming up to his side.

In the darkness before them, there was a deeper darkness that bore the indistinct appearance of a human form, lying in a stooping posture close to the trunk of the tree.

A vague presentiment of the truth flashed upon the mind of the Virginian, who enjoining silence on his companion, advanced close to the object, and laid his hand upon it. There could be no longer a doubt. The blanket coat, and woollen sash, which he first touched, and then the shoe pack, told him in unmistakable language that it was Le Noir, the Canadian owner of the dog. He shook him, and twice, in a low voice called him by name. But there was no answer, while the body stiff and motionless, fully revealed the fate of the unfortunate man.

Meanwhile, Loup Garou, which had followed, squatted himself at the head, which was hanging over the front of what they knew, from its handles and the peculiar odor, exhaling from it, to be a wheel-barrow filled with manure, and then commenced licking--moaning at the same time in a low and broken whine.

"What can the dog mean by that?" whispered Weston.

"Don't you hear him licking his dead master's face, and telling his sorrow in his own way," answered the corporal as, in order to assure himself, he dropped his hand to the mouth of the dog; but no sooner had he done so, than he drew it suddenly back with a shudder of disgust and hastily wiped it, clammy with the blood that yet trickled from the scalped head of the murdered man.

A low whistle was here given on the left, and a few yards above, that startled the Virginian, for it was the signal agreed upon if anything suspicious, should be noticed by the other parties. He promptly answered it in a different call, and in another minute Green and Philips had joined him. "What have you seen?" he inquired, not regarding the exclamation of surprise of the new comers, at the unexpected sight before them.

"We've seen nothin' its so dark," answered Green, "but unless the cattle have got into the garden, there's somethin' else movin' there. Philips and I listened after we heard the dog howl the first time, for we could hear as if somethin' like steps were stopped suddenly when he moaned the second time we listened again, and thought the same thing."

"They couldn't be cattle," added Philips, "for the cattle are all kept on the other side."

"Only the young stock, and them as ain't used about the farm," remarked Weston.

"Well, but what kind of steps were they?" eagerly questioned the corporal, whose, imagination was filled not more with the danger that seemed to be near them, than with the censure of himself he feared he should incur, on his return to the fort, for having subjected the party to risk. "Surely you can tell between the tread of cattle and the steps of men."

"I should say they, weren't the steps of cattle; they were too light for that. Though they couldn't help crushin' the dry sticks and rubbish they couldn't help seein' lyin' in the way. Don't you think so Philips?"

"I did, corporal, and so sure did I guess them to be no cattle that it was me that whistled."

"Then there's no use in going farther," remarked the Virginian gravely. "Even if we get to the house, we can't see anything in it for the darkness, and the poor fellow shows plain enough that it's to use looking out to save Mr. Heywood or Ephraim Giles. Come, my lads, we must get back to the boat, and down stream as quick and as quiet as we can."

Giving his own low whistle of recall, he was answered from the opposite direction, and in a few minutes Cass and Jackson made their appearance.

These latter were, briefly questioned whether they had seen anything, and great was the anxiety of all when it was known that they had also heard in the orchard but in a fainter manner, what had attracted the attention of Green and Philips in the garden.

"Why didn't you give the signal then, as directed?"

"Because," answered Cass, "We weren't quite sure about it, and feared the whistle might tell the Injins, if any were near, our whereabouts."

Scarce had this explanation been given, when the attention of all was arrested by a loud clear shout of the corporals' name, evidently uttered by Collins.

"Into the house--into the house," exclaimed the same voice. "The Injins are creeping up to you."

As these words came ringing upon the silence of the night the dull steps in rapid advance through the two enclosures were now distinctly heard, while the flash of a gun fired in their rear, lighted up the forms of three or four savages, gliding up to them by the pathway by which the corporal had come.

The danger was imminent, the necessity for securing the important position imperative, and without waiting for the order of their superior, or even uttering a word, the whole of the party, acting upon the caution of Collins, made a rush towards the front entrance of the house, which they gained at the very moment when the rattling of the snake-fences, and the total overthrow of the slight enclosure, announced that their enemies were thus near in pursuit.

Fortunately the door was wide open, so that they had all passed in, when the Indians on either flank, as though by previous arrangement, poured in their cross fire, towards that common centre, without, however, striking anything but the logs.

Terrific and continuous yells succeeded, and well was it that, with cool promptitude, the corporal had sought, and found behind the door, where he knew they were usually kept, the strong bars, three in number, that secured the heavy panels, for as many of the Indians as could find room to act together, now applied their shoulders to the frame with such violence, that but for those timely safeguards, it must have yielded. During more than five minutes they persevered in their efforts, the men waiting anxiously in attitude of preparation for the result, when all at once they ceased, and their footsteps were heard cautiously retiring.

"Quick, look to the back-door, two of you," commanded the corporal in an eager, but low tone, "they are going round; there, if that is not secured we are lost."

Green and Philips sprang forward towards the point indicated, but the latter in his excitement stumbled heavily against something, and fell at his length upon the floor, exclaiming: "I've fallen over a dead man, and am half drowned in his blood."

His companion who had escaped this obstruction, had scarcely time to assure the corporal that the back door was already barred, a fact which he had discovered by dint of feeling, when the latch was first heard gently tried, then the door violently assaulted. Another loud and angry yell from the Indians announced their disappointment, then several shots were fired at the door, and two or three balls could be heard dropping and rolling upon the floor, after having passed through the heavy planks.

"Safe enough now for a while, my lads," said the corporal exultingly, "and we can have, a little breathing time. Who's got the means of striking a light, that we may see where we are, and what we're about?"

"I have," answered Green, as taking a flint, steel, and tinder from his pocket, he, with a couple of strokes, ignited the latter, and approached the hearth, which the faint light from the burning "punk" enabled him to reach. The fire had long since gone out, but the crisp and blackened embers, soon grew under the care of the soldier into light sufficient to render objects in the apartment gradually more and more distinguishable.

While this process was going on, the rest, leaning on their muskets, were anxiously grouped around the spot where Philips had fallen. At first, only the outline of a man of large stature and proportions could be seen lying in a cramped position, as if produced by some strong convulsive agony, and then when the fire began to kindle and crackle, the dress could be distinguished, and then as the light grew brighter, the scalpless head, and then the marked and distorted features of the murdered master of the house, who lay in a pool of blood that slowly trickled along the crevices of the floor. His hands were firmly clenched upon the barrel of a rifle which had been broken off at the stock, that now lay a few yards beyond, while the features, sternly set in death, bore a mingled expression of defiance and resolution. A cut, as from a tomahawk had laid open his left temple, while on several parts of his body could be seen thick encrustations of blood that had exuded through the rent clothing, marking the seat of several stabs and gunshot wounds. It was evident that Mr. Heywood had not lost his life without a desperate, struggle, for independently of the testimony afforded by his broken rifle, which he seemed to have used with fierce determination, the heavy table had been overthrown, and the few articles of necessary furniture in the room evidently displaced.

"What a tale, this, to carry back," gravely remarked Weston. "I wouldn't take the corporal's stripes to-morrow, and be the first man to tell Miss Heywood of it."

"Supposing we get back at all," said Cass. "Though we're safe enough for the present, I've no notion these devils will let us off go soon."

"There's no great danger now," interrupted the corporal. "I defy them, if they're not stronger than we saw them this morning, to get into the house, with six good firelocks to defend it."

"But they may set fire to it, and burn us out," persevered the apprehensive man with the hooked nose and the peaked chin; "I've heard of those things before."

"Burn your granny out, Nutcrackers; look at them logs well, and say if it would'nt take hell-fire itself to burn 'em through in a month, but corporal, had'nt we better divide the ammunition. We don't know, as Cass says, what the imps are about, and what trouble they may give us yet."

"Right, Green, there's nothing like being on the sure side, and so, my lads look to the pouches. Weston, there's a candle in that stone bottle on the shelf--light it, and put it on the table as soon as you have got that on its legs again."

The examination was soon made. Each small cartouch box, expressly made for light excursions, contained, with the exception of the single cartridge which Collins had fired, the usual allowance of fifteen rounds. Two of these however--those of Green and Philips--had been so saturated by long immersion in the water, that they were wholly unserviceable. They were therefore emptied and dried, and the deficiency supplied from the pouches of their comrades, thus leaving about a dozen charges to each man.

"A small stock of ammunition, this, I guess, to stand a long siege on an empty belly," drawled forth Cass.

"Just like you--always croakin'," sneered Green, "and always thinking of your belly. Why man, you've more ammunition there, I take it, than ever you'll fire away in your life."

"And if we haven't enough," said the corporal, going to, and taking down and shaking a powder horn, which hung suspended from the wall, that had evidently been overlooked by the Indians, "here are a dozen more charges at least, and the balls of the cartridges have not, I take it, lost their power to drill a hole into a fellow because they've been considerably well ducked. But hark! what noise is that--listen!"

A low, grating sound, as of some heavy body rubbing against the ground, was now audible at short intervals, to seemed to proceed from the southern gable--but not a voice was heard. From the moment when they had uttered their cry of disappointment, on finding the back entrance secured, the Indians had preserved the utmost silence.

Suddenly a yell, pealed from the direction of the river, caused them for the first time to revert to the exposed position of the unfortunate Collins.

"Poor fellow," said Green, dashing away a tear. "I wish he was with us. Somehow or other, I feel as if we should all have a better chance in a fight, were that lad in the middle of it."

"We shall never see him more!" gravely observed the Virginian; "That shot fired just after he warned us, did his business, depend upon it, and if that one didn't, it is not likely the blood-hounds would let him off after robbing them of their prey: no, no, poor Collins has lost his life in saving us."

Again the yell was repeated, and from the same quarter. The corporal sprang to the ladder which communicated with the loft, and having placed it under the window on the front, hastily ascended and looked out, for no one had hitherto thought of closing an opening, from which no danger was, seemingly, to be apprehended.

The darkness which had been so excessive at the moment of their entrance, had greatly diminished--so much so, that he could trace the forms of two or three of the warriors who were stooping low, apparently engaged with some object lying on the very bank of the river.

"Scalping and mutilating the poor fellow, no doubt," he muttered fiercely to himself, "but here goes to revenge him!"

Forgetting his usual prudence, he, in the strong excitement of the moment, drew up the butt of his musket to his shoulder, and as well as his cramped position would permit, covered one of the savages, but while in the very act of pulling the trigger, they all fell prostrate, and the bullet whizzed harmlessly over them. In the next instant a ball, aimed at himself, and fired from another quarter, passed through the window, grazing the shoulder slightly bitten by Loup Garou, and lodged in the opposite logs of the room. A third loud yell followed as the corporal drew in his head and disappeared from the window. The Indians evidently thought he had been hit, and thus gave utterance to their triumph.

"There's that grating sound again," remarked Weston.

All now listened, and heard much more distinctly than before the peculiar sound. Then followed a scratching and bumping of something heavy against the end of the house.

"I have it," said the Virginian. "They've dragged the ladder from the barn, and are trying to fix it under the bedroom window. Cass, do you and Philips go in and see what they're doing. But close the door after you that they may not pick you off by the light."

The door was cautiously opened and again shut as soon as the men had entered. They looked up at the window, which, in the darkness that prevailed around, was distinctly enough visible, but although open, nothing met their glance of a nature to startle them, nor could any movement be heard without.

"Hold my firelock," whispered Cass to his companion, "while I try and get a look out. I know poor Le Noir's bed is directly under the window, and I don't think THAT is too high, if I stand on the pillow."

He now cautiously groped his way to the bed, on ascending which, being a tall man, he found the top of his head to be on a level with the sill of the window. This was not sufficient for his purpose, and he sought to elevate himself still more. In attempting, with this view, to place himself on the head-board, he missed his footing, and fell with some force between the head of the bed, and the rode log wall. To his dismay, he found that his feet had rested not upon the hard floor of the apartment, but upon something soft and yielding, which his imagination, strongly excited by the events of the day, led him unhesitatingly to conclude, was the flesh of a human body.

"A light corporal--a light!" he shouted, regardless of every thing, but his desire to release himself from his present situation. "Bring a light. Here's a fellow, who has got hold of me by the leg!"

"Take your musket then and bayonet him," said Philips, coolly, as he pushed towards the struggling man the butt end of his firelock, which at length reached his hands. At the same time, Corporal Nixon, rendered equally imprudent by the suddenness of the demand for his presence, entered, followed by Weston, bearing the candle.

CHAPTER VI.

Nothing can, we conceive, be in worse taste in a fictitious narrative, than the wanton introduction of the ludicrous upon the solemn, but when in an historical tale these extremes do occur, fidelity forbids the suppression of the one, lest it should mar the effect of the other. Such is the necessity under which we find ourselves.

The first act of the corporal, on seeing how matters stood, was to pull back the bedstead behind which Cass was imprisoned, so as wholly to uncover him and his assailant, but the surprise of all may be imagined, when, instead of an Indian, with whom they believed him to be struggling, they beheld an immense turkey-cock, well known to them all, which was partly under the foot of the soldier--partly in a boarded drain or reservoir which passed from the apartment into a large hog trough, that lay along the wall and daily received the refuse of the various meals. The bird, furious with pain, was burying its beak into the leg of the soldier, while he, with the butt end of his musket aloft, and the bayonet depressed, offered the most burlesque representation of St. George preparing to give his mortal thrust to the dragon.

In spite of the danger by which they were beset, it was impossible for the men to restrain the indulgence of their humor at this singular sight, nor was the disposition at all checked, when they saw the bayonet descend and actually transfix the intruder to the floor-causing him to droop his head, and thus free Cass from his furious attacks.

"If that's the way you kill your enemies, Nutcrackers, we promise to eat them up for you--as many as you like," and as he spoke, Green advanced and seized the dying bird by the throat; but as he pulled it suddenly away, a dark human hand was observed to relinquish its hold of the feet, and rapidly disappear.

The mirth of the men was now succeeded by a seriousness befitting the occasion, for it was clear to all that this occurrence, absurd as it was, had been the means of betraying a new plan of the enemy to get into the house. If the drain was large enough to admit of the passage of the bird--always remarkable for its size--it was highly possible that some of the more slightly formed Indians, might force their way through it also. They had evidently tried to see if it could be done--the turkey-cock having been put forward as a "feeler," and the necessity of either closing the avenue, or weakening their strength by keeping a man constantly on the watch, was now obvious.

"Find something to stop up that hole with Cass," ordered the corporal.

"I can see nothing," replied the other, after a few moments search, unless we stop it with the bedding."

"A wise plan that. The Injins would soon set fire to it, and if they didn't burn us out, they would soon smoke us out. Either would suit their purpose."

"Let him stuff it with his head, corporal," interposed Green, "I'm sure that's thick enough for a plug."

"Perhaps there's a head in it already," suggested Philips, "there was a hand just now--the other may have followed."

"By jingo I'll try," returned Green, "I'd give a week's grog to be able to prick a feller with this playthin'"

So saying, he knelt upon the floor, and holding his musket in a horizontal position, a few inches above it, he gave a furious thrust into the aperture. To his astonishment, for notwithstanding his half bravado, he had not seriously anticipated such a result, he found the advance of his weapon slightly arrested by a yielding body, and even had not a sharp cry of pain from the other extremity of the trough, satisfied him of the fact, the peculiar sensation he experienced as the steel overcame the resistance was sufficient to convince Green, little accustomed even as he had been to bayonet men, that the bayonet had entered into some soft part of the human body.

To the cry of the wounded man, succeeded a savage and threatening yell from the united band, and now re-commenced the grating sound which had two or three times before excited the conjectures of the besieged.

"Ah I yell away you devils; that's all the good you'll get," exclaimed Green, exulting at his success; "but don't take so tight a grip of my bayonet. I say, Philips, lend us a hand, if I shan't lose my musket with that fellow strugglin' like a speared Mascalinga."

Both now pulled at the firelock, with all their strength. Suddenly the resistance ceased, and they fell sideways on the floor, bringing the musket with them, but without the bayonet. At the same moment a shot was fired into the aperture, and the ball whizzing by the ear of Philips, and passing through Green's right leg, lodged in the partition beyond.

"Stand aside, men," shouted the corporal, "stand from before that hole, or we shall be marks in this light for the skulking villains,"

Jackson, who had been dispatched for one of the small round hickory logs that lay piled up in a corner near the chimney, now approached with on that was just large enough to fit tightly in the aperture. All seized it, and taking the precaution to keep their legs out of danger, jammed one end into the mouth of the drain, adding afterwards a few heavy blows from the axes of Le Noir and Ephraim Giles, which had been found in a corner of the room.

"Now then," said the Virginian, after having examined the small window of the bed room, and securely fastened the shutter--"we've not much more to fear. They're two to one its true, but I defy them to do us much harm before daylight, when, I take it they'll be off, if not sooner."

"Well, then, corporal," suggested Green, "I vote that as we're pretty safe, and have yet that piece of plunder, we set to work and cook it, for I'm devilish hungry, and so I think we must all be, seeing as how we hain't had a regular meal the whole day, besides if we rummage the place, we may chance to light upon somethin' else. I see the varmint have carried off the nice row of venison hams that used to hang up round the chimney, but there may be somethin' in the loft."

"No bad thought that of yours, Green," answered the corporal, "Cass, you killed the bird, you must pluck it and grill it."

"That's what I call taking it sensibly," said the latter leaning his musket against the wall, and dragging the heavy turkey to the kitchen-corner, where seated on the very chair on which poor Mr. Heywood had smoked his last pipe, he commenced plucking out the feathers by handfuls. "Let fasting without, and feasting within be the word; but its mortal dry eating that great he turkey, without something to wash it down. I say, Philips, you are a good hand at foraging--don't you think you could find out a little of the Wabash there," and he pointed to the loft.

Philips approached the ladder with the intention of making a search, but the Virginian checked him.

"Stop a moment," he said, "until I have had another look out in front." Thus saying he cautiously ascended to his former position, the view from which was much less indistinct than before. The obscurity had, in a great degree, passed away, so much so, that all objects within the area formed by the enclosures of the garden and the orchard were thrown into perceptible relief. His first thought was to cast his glance upon the water, hoping, he scarcely knew why, that something might be seen of the skiff which had contained the unfortunate Collins. Disappointed in that quarter, his eye next turned upon the walnut tree, the white blossoms of which had dropped around and upon the spot, where lay the body of the ill-fated Le Noir, at whose head was still squatted, as when he had left him, his faithful dog. There was much in this trait of devotion on the part of the animal which could not fail to awaken sympathy even in the roughest heart, and although the corporal was not particularly sentimental, he could not but be deeply touched by the contrast forced upon him, between the moaning animal and the wild lust for blood which reigned in the hearts of their unprovoked assailants. His first impulse was to call approvingly to the dog, but the next moment's reflection on the folly of such a proceeding stifled the impulse. Then his attention was called not only to the perfect immunity from further outrage of the victim and his follower, but to the profound silence, and absence of danger which seemed to exist in that quarter. That the Indians had not departed, although they had not been heard since the yell that followed the cry produced by the thrust from Green's bayonet, he felt confident, and it now seemed to him that they must be directing their efforts against some other part of the building.

No sooner had he admitted this last belief, than he again descended, and raising the ladder himself, bore it noiselessly to the spot whence it had been removed, then ordering the candle to be extinguished, and the embers to be drawn together, so as to deaden the light of the fire, he with Green and Weston crept up the ladder, Cass being left to complete the preparation of the turkey the best way he could, while Philips and Jackson, posted at the back and front doors, listened attentively for the slightest sound of danger, which being heard, they were at once to warn the party above.

When the corporal had gained the top of the ladder, Green, who was the last, having yet his foot on the first step, the former was evidently startled by some new danger. But just as he was in the act of springing to the upper floor, the ladder, too frail to sustain their united weight, snapped suddenly asunder in the middle and fell with some noise, thus separating him from his companions.

Regardless of this and having secured his own footing, he now moved cautiously towards the opposite end of the loft, where a small opening, about two feet in length, and one in height, seemingly intended as a ventilator, appeared nearly vertical to the window of the bed-room below. Casting his glance downwards through the opening, he beheld five or six savages standing grouped together, leaning on their guns, and apparently watching some object above them. This, naturally, drew the corporal's attention to the same quarter, when to his dismay he found that the long ladder usually kept at the barn was now resting against the gable of the house, not three feet from the right corner of the aperture, through which he gazed. In an instant it occurred to him that this had been the work of the Indians, and at once accounted for the grating sounds that had so often met his ears that night. There could be no doubt that the plan of the enemy now was to enter the roof, which could be done by removing part of the raw buffalo hides of which it was composed. Indeed it was a slight noise made in the direction of that very angle of the roof where the ladder now stood, that had caught his attention on first putting his head through the aperture while preceding his men. This had suddenly ceased at the moment when the ladder broke and fell, nor had there been a repetition of the sound. Still, satisfied that some discovery of the true designs of the Indians would result from his remaining a little longer, he continued at the opening, which was too small to betray his presence if using precaution, while it enabled him to observe the movements of the enemy. Soon afterwards he heard them speaking in earnest but low tones, as if addressing somebody above them, and then a prolonged yell, which was answered by others from the front of the house, echoed through the surrounding forests. Even amid the horrid discord, the quick ear of the Virginian, now painfully on the stretch, caught the same sound that had first attracted his attention. It was exactly at the angle of the roof, and only a pace or two from him. The peculiar noise was not to be mistaken even by an unpractised ear. It was, evidently, that of a knife, not very sharp, cautiously cutting through a tough and resisting leather.

The corporal became now more anxious than ever, but this feeling did not in the slightest degree, disturb his self-possession, or cause him to waver in the resolution he had from the first adopted. He waited patiently, until, as he expected, he heard a corner of one of the buffalo hides turned up, and beheld reflected, against the back-ground of light, thus suddenly introduced, the upper part of a human being, whose shorn head, covered on the crown with straight and slightly streaming feathers, too plainly indicated his purpose. What a target for the bullet--what an object for the bayonet of the soldier, who, had not prudence and coolness interposed, had certainly used one or the other. But the Virginian had hit upon another, and as he conceived, a better plan to get rid of his enemy, and in his fate, of further probable annoyance from his ferocious companions. It was not his object to let himself be seen, or that the Indians should even suspect that they had been detected in this new device, for he was well aware that if he fired, or used his bayonet against the man, those below would rush up the ladder to succeed him, and by their weight prevent the accomplishment of what he had in view; therefore cut off as he in a measure was, from his party, it was incumbent on him to adopt the only sure means of relief from danger, and that without a moment of delay.

While the Indian, who finding, evidently, that the orifice he had made in the roof was not yet large enough for his purpose, had dropped the incised portion of the hide, and was again using his knife; the Virginian, stooping slightly at the off-side of the window, ascertained that the feet of the former were resting on one of the upper steps of the ladder. This was what he desired, and all he now wanted was a hard, flat substance to fasten on the point of his bayonet. After reflecting vainly for a few moments how this was to be attained, he suddenly bethought him of his thick-soled ammunition-boots. Removing one of these without noise, he pierced the inner leather, by pressing it firmly against the point of the bayonet, so as to secure without allowing it to pass through. Then, cautiously protruding his musket from the opening, he slowly advanced it, until the sole of the boot touched the frame of the ladder, not two feet under the round on which the Indian stood. Here for a moment he allowed the barrel, concealed by the low depending eaves, to rest against the jamb of the aperture. His anxiety was now worked up to the highest possible pitch, for he feared, notwithstanding his success so far, that something might yet occur to defeat his purpose, and thus peril not only his own life, but the lives of the whole of the party below. Three minutes he remained in this trying position of uncertainty, which seemed to him as so many hours. Presently, however, the Indian on the roof, having evidently accomplished his task, and believing from the silence that had for some time pervaded around, that no one was near him, spoke in a low tone to his companions, who now cautiously crept towards the ladder.

This was the moment for action. The Virginian, who, although expecting this, had watched their movements with aching interest, now summoned his whole strength, and while the first savage below was upon the ladder, pushed his musket with such violence against the sole, that it carried it rapidly over the corner of the house, before the Indian could find presence of mind to throw himself upon the roof--a sudden backward jerk of the weapon liberated the bayonet, the extreme point of which only had entered the wood, and as the Virginian withdrew this, he could distinctly see the unfortunate savages fall headlong from the top of the ladder, uttering, as both descended, a fearful cry of dismay, which was responded to by fierce yells from the lips of their companions, who hastened to their succor.

"Well done, that!" said the corporal, exultingly, and half-aloud to himself, as he slapped his thigh, in a manner to denote his own self-approval. "That's what I call doing the business as it should be done. The attempt," and he smiled at the conceit, "was not a bootless one to us all, though it has been a BOOT LESS one to ME."

To understand this facetiousness of the Virginian, it must be understood that on withdrawing his bayonet, the boot which it had only slightly pierced, had slipped from the weapon and fallen to the ground simultaneously with the other heavier bodies, whose more marked sound had absorbed its own. It therefore escaped the notice of the Indians.

"Hilloa there!" he continued in a louder key; "there's no more danger in this quarter, my lads. Show us a light, and if Cass has that turkey ready, we'll have some supper. For my part, I'm devilish sharp set. Here, Green, take my musket, and give me the candle."

Surprised at the corporal's unwonted humor, for they had been led to apprehend, from the noise made by the falling ladder, and the excitement evidently prevailing among the Indians, that some new act of treachery was about to be tried by them, the men gathered underneath the opening, Green taking his musket from the hands of the Virginian, while in return, he mounted on one of the low chairs, and extending his arm far above, handed him the light.

After a few minutes search, the corporal appeared again at the mouth of the loft, not only with a demijohn half-filled with whisky, but with a large loaf of brown bread, and part of a shoulder of dried venison, from which nearly one-half had been chipped away in slices. This, indeed, was a prize, and the men looked at the articles of necessary supply, as they were successively handed down, with an earnestness which denoted, that whatever might be their apprehensions of danger from without, they by no means coveted fighting on an empty stomach. After having lowered the treasures he had been so fortunate as to secure, the Virginian swung himself down by his hands, without difficulty, upon the lower floor.

The fire had been again revived, and having ordered Jackson up into the loft, to keep watch at the small-window, and apprise him if any attempt should be made to replace the ladder, the corporal for the first time lighting his pipe, sat down to ruminate on his position, and consider the means by which the party were to be taken back to the fort. Further serious apprehensions in regard to their safety he did not now entertain, for baulked, as the Indians had been, in all their attempts to get into the house, he felt persuaded that it was more with a view to annoy and alarm, than with any hope of eventual success, that they still lingered in the neighborhood. Had they been in a situation to continue the siege longer than the morning, the case might have been different. But it was obvious that in order to secure their own safety, alarmed as they most know the governor would be at the absence of the party under his command, they would not remain longer than daylight exposed to the chances of being themselves closely assailed from without.

Such was the reasoning of the Virginian, whose greatest source of discomfort now was the apprehension of serious reprimand, if not something worse, from the austere Captain Headley, whose displeasure, he was certain, would be so much the greater on account of the loss of the unfortunate Collins. He looked at his watch, but to his great annoyance, found that it had stopped, the hour-hand pointing to one o'clock. How long it had been run down, he could not tell, but from the time which had elapsed since their abandonment of the boat, and arrival in the house, he did not think it could be less than four in the morning.

Desirous to satisfy himself by the appearance of the heavens, he arose, and with the aid of Green, placed the table under the window commanding a view of the river. This being too low, a chair was placed upon it, thus affording the corporal the advantage of greater elevation than he had derived from the use of the ladder itself.

Everything was again quiet. Not a sound broke the stillness, save the howling of a few wolves, which, probably, attracted by the scent of the human blood that had been spilt that day, and by the exposed corpse that was now strewed with white blossoms from the tree beneath which it lay, were, by the increasing light, indistinctly seen on the opposite shore. But not their savage cry of hunger alone was heard. Ever and anon, in reply to their fierce howling was heard the snappish bark of Loup Garou, as, leaping on the body of his unconscious master, he lashed his tail, and seemed to bid defiance to those whose errand he seemed so perfectly to divine.

"Poor dog! you shall never want a master while I can keep you," half murmured the corporal, as he now turned his gaze upon the water, anxious to see if any trace could be found there of the skiff and its missing occupant. Nothing, however, came within his view, but just as he was preparing to descend from the window, the outline of the boat, for from its peculiar shape he easily identified it as their own, riveted his attention as it passed quickly up the river, filled with seven or eight savages in their war-dress, and having at the bow what had the appearance of a pole, from the top of which dangled a human scalp.

"Gone at last," he exclaimed, after a moment's pause, "but with poor Collins' scalp along with them. Cass," he added, as he sprang to the floor, "if that turkey is fit to eat let's have it directly, and you, Weston, look about and see if there is any more water to be had. Make haste, now, for we shall have to tramp it to the fort as soon as it's daylight. The devils are gone and carried off the boat."

Not less anxious than himself to be once more on their way to the fort, which some of them, on entering the house that night, had scarcely hoped to reach alive, the men, leaning their muskets against the side of the room, assisted in preparing the rude, but grateful meal, of which they stood so much in need, and which was to sustain them during the short-approaching march. The table having been placed in the centre of the room, and on it the demijohn, and bread and venison, Green and Weston, the latter of whom had been unsuccessful in his search for water, seized each a leg and a wing of the ample turkey, which now denuded and disembowelled, Cass had scientifically carved in its raw state, and held them in the blaze of the fire, waiting patiently until the blackness of the outside should give promise of corresponding warmth within. Its slayer held the body of the bird over the fire in a similar manner, the poker having been thrust into the abdomen. They all sat, or rather stood in a squatting position with their faces to the fire.

"Well, now, I reckon we shall make six considerable shares of this," drawled Cass, looking fondly at the carcass, which was slowly but temptingly spluttering before him at the fire. "Are you any ways particular, Green?--what part suits your taste best, Weston--a leg or a wing? For my part I always stick to the carcass."

"Faith, and I like both, and a slice of the breast to boot. I'm just the fellow, now the varmints are gone, that could eat all of them."

"Yes, but you know," returned the temporary chef de cuisine, "it must be share and share alike--there's two legs--two wings and the breast, and the back slit in two--that just makes six portions, and we're six men in all."

"Cast lots fiddlestick," said Green, "what portion do you expect, Nutcrackers? unless it's the neck, and the scaly part of the leg, the Injin had hold of when you so bravely sent your bayonet through her feathers."

"Well, only think how cunning of the fellows," remarked Weston, "who'd ever have thought they would try that fashion to get in, cramming an old turkey before them to clear the way, and get in his craw the first bullet that might be sent."

"Yes, and the tight grip the fellow had of him by the leg. Just look, Green, the mark of the devil's hand may be upon him yet. It was the right leg, and that's it you have."

"Bosh! what do you expect me to find there but the marks of your dirty paws while plucking him, I'm too devilish hungry for such nonsense, Nutcrackers; but show me the Injin that would venture to touch his legs now. If I wouldn't mark him, then my name's not Seth Green."

Scarcely had he finished speaking, when a dark naked human hand was slowly protruded over his shoulder, and seized not the leg of the turkey, which Green now grasped with unconscious and convulsive energy, but a brand from the fire.

In his terror at that strange and unexpected appearance, he dropped the body of the bird in the glowing embers, and uttering a faint cry, turned half round and beheld what filled him with the deepest dismay: his companions, scarcely less terrified than himself, sprang together to their feet, with the intention of rushing to their muskets, but all hope of recovering them was gone. The savage who had snatched the fire was no longer there then, but half a dozen others in their war-paint stood between them and their firelocks. It seemed as if they were sensible that their very silence inspired more awe and apprehension in the bosoms of their defenceless enemies than could have done the most turbulent expression of their triumph. They had evidently entered by the back door, which was now quite open, and grouped around the body of Mr. Heywood, were apparently more interested in the dead than in the living. Not a sign was there of the corporal, and Philips stood as if paralyzed, leaning, musket in hand, against the opposite entrance.

CHAPTER VII.

Leaving the little party in the dismay occasioned by their new position, and that at a moment when they believed themselves secured from further interruption or danger, we must now return to the Fort, where their long-continued absence, coupled with the startling tidings conveyed by Ephraim Giles, had created equal anxiety and apprehension.

It will be recollected that during the examination of the latter, Ensign Ronayne had, after communicating with the commanding officer, suddenly departed across the river, taking with him a few armed men. The destination of this little party was the cottage occupied by Mrs. Heywood and her daughter, who, with a woman servant, were the sole occupants of a dwelling, simple in construction, but decorated, both within and without, by the hand of good taste. It was a low, one-storied building, painted white, with green window-blinds and shutters, and a verandah of trellis work of the same color, that extended a few feet square round the principal entrance. On either side, rose to the roof, on parallel lines, and at equal distances, cords of strong twine, on which already had began to interlace themselves, the various parasites indigenous to the soil, which winter had robbed of their freshness, but which a southern sun was now evidently vivifying and re-invigorating. A small garden of about half-an-acre, surrounded by a similar trellis-work, extended equally in front, and on the sides of the house--while the graceful form given to the various beds, and the selection of the plants and flowers, which, although still in their dormant state, were yet recognizable--testified the refined taste of those who had assisted at their culture. The pathway, which was recently gravelled from the adjacent sand-hills, ran in a straight line from the verandah, toward the little green gate, opening on the front of the garden, took a semi-circular sweep on either side, at about one-third of the distance from the gate. This form had been given to it for the purpose of affording room for the creation of a mound, on the summit of which had been placed a small summer-house, octagon in shape, and constructed of the same description of trellis-work. The sloping sides of the mound itself, were profusely covered with dahlias, rhododendrons, geraniums, and other plants of the most select kind--the whole forming, when in bloom, a circle of floral magnificence. A short and narrow path, just large enough to admit of the passage of one person at a time, led to the entrance of the summer-house, which, facing the gate, was also shaded from the light and heat of the sun's rays, by closely interlacing vines.

At the bottom of this artificial mound, and near the pathway, a small spud, such as is used for pruning, was stuck into some earth, newly drawn round a splendid tiger lily, and on the handle of the spud, were loosely thrown a white silk jacket, a blue velvet cap, and a light pink scarf--evidencing that no ordinary gardener had been that day employed in bringing into new life the gorgeous beauties of the var-iegated parterre.

"Little did I think," mused the young officer, as, leaving his party at the, gate, and hastening towards the cottage, his eye fell upon those articles of dress--"little did I imagine when I threw off these things a few hours since, to obey a summons to the Fort, that on my return to them, it would be with this heavy heart, and as the bearer of these tidings--but I must be cautious in my disclosure. Dear girl, here she is!"

"Why, Ronayne, what in the name of Heaven is the meaning of all this? Are you here to take the castle by storm, with all these armed warriors? A few hours since you were a man of peace, and now I behold in you a most approved and valiant knight of the true American school. Sword, cap, feather, epaulet, blue broad-cloth, and silver. Well it must be confessed that you are not a bad imitation of a soldier, in that garb, and it is in pity to me, I suppose, that you do not wear it oftener. But seriously, Harry, do satisfy my curiosity, and tell me the reason of this unusual--manner of visit!"

The question was asked playfully, but in tones replete with sweetness, by a tall and elegantly-formed girl, who on turning the further circle of the walk, in her ap-proach to her favorite flower-bed, had for the first time, beheld the young officer, and the party stationed at the gate.

"Nay, dear Maria," returned the youth, deeply grieved at the thought of casting a gloom over the spirits of her who thus rallied him. "I am sorry to say my errand is not one of mere parade--I have come to announce that which will give you pain; and but that I am charged with the agreeable duty of making you a prisoner, I never should have had the courage to be the bearer of the intelligence."

Miss Heywood turned very pale, less at the words even than at the manner of the young officer, who it was evident, felt all the weight of the task he had undertaken.

"Ronayne," she said, her voice suddenly assuming a rich melancholy of intonation, in strange contrast with her first address, "there is more in this than you would acquaint me with. But, tell me," and she fixed her large dark eyes on his--"tell me all. What pain is it you fear to occasion me, and how is it connected with my being a prisoner? Ha!" and she grasped his arm, and betrayed deep agitation--"surely nothing in my father's conduct--"

"No, no, Maria," returned the youth, quickly, "far from anything of the kind, and yet it is of your father I would speak. But have you heard nothing since I left you. Have you seen no one?"

"I have heard nothing--seen not a soul from without," she answered, as he tenderly pressed the hand he had taken--"But, Ronayne," she pursued, with melancholy gravity--"a sudden light dawns upon me--my heart tells me that some misfortune or other has happened, or is about to happen--you say you would speak about my father. You are the bearer of ill-news in regard to him. Yes, I know it is so; tell me, Harry," and she looked imploringly up to him, "am I not right?--my father has been attacked by Indians, and he has fallen. Oh! you do not deny it!"

"Nay, dearest Maria, I know nothing of the kind, although I will not conceal from you that there is danger--you have guessed correctly as to the Indians having been at the farm, but little certain is known as to the result of their visit. That half idiot Ephraim Giles, has come in with some wild story, but I daresay he exaggerates."

Miss Heywood shook her head doubtingly. "You deceive me, Ronayne--with the best intention, but still you deceive me. If you really think the rumor be exaggerated, why your own restlessness and seriousness of manner? Harry, this is no time for concealment, for I feel that I can better bear the truth NOW than LATER. Do not hesitate then to tell me all you know."

"True, my love, this is no time for concealment since such be the state of your feelings. I was unwilling to admit my own apprehension on the subject, fearing that you might be ill-prepared for the disclosure; but after what you have just urged, the blow can never fall less heavily than now. You must know, then, that a party of hostile Indians have, there is too much reason to fear, used violence toward the inmates of the farm-house, but to what extent we have no means of knowing; though such is the alarm created by their presence that Headley, who you know is the very soul of caution, has ordered every white in the neighborhood of the Fort, to be removed for safety within its walls."

"Would that instead of THAT," remarked Miss Heywood, with solemnity, "he had despatched those soldiers, whom I see there fully armed, to the rescue of my poor father. Perhaps he might be saved yet--the house is strong, and might be defended for some time, even by a couple of men."

"And me at their head. Is it not so, Maria?" inquired the youth.

"Yes, and you at their head, dear Ronayne," repeated Miss Heywood; "to no one sooner would I be indebted for my father's safety, as no one would, I am sure, more cheerfully attempt his deliverance."

The young American mused a moment, and then rejoined, despondingly; "Were these men at my disposal, Maria, how gladly would I hasten to encounter every difficulty, the removal of which would spare your gentle bosom those pangs; but you know Headley would never permit it. His prudence is a mania, and even were he to yield his consent--let me not sustain you with delusive hopes--I fear it would be too late."

"God's will be done," she ejaculated, as the large tears fell trickling down her pallid cheeks, "but what will become of my poor and now nearly death-stricken-mother, when she hears of this?"

"The blow is indeed a fearful one, but act, I pray you, with courage. Consider, too, your own safety. No one knows the force of the Indians, or how soon they may be here. Go in, dearest, prepare what you may more immediately require for a few days, and my men will carry your trunks down to the scow which is waiting to receive you."

"And if I should consent to go, Ronayne, you know my poor mother cannot rise from her bed. What do you propose to do with her? To remove her, and let her know WHY she is removed, would soon finish the work her debilitating disease has begun."

"I have made every necessary provision," answered the young officer, glad to find that her thoughts could be diverted from the immediate source of her sorrow. "Elmsley's wife, to whom I spoke a few hurried words on leaving, is even now preparing for your temporary reception, and I have thought of an excuse to be given to your mother. You must for once in your life use deceit, and say that Van Vottenberg desires her presence in the fort, because his duties have become so severe that he can no longer absent himself to bestow upon her that professional care she so much requires. Nay, look not so incredulous. I am aware that the pretext is a meagre one, but I cannot at present think of a better; and in her enfeebled state she will not dwell upon the strangeness of the plea. Go on then, I entreat you, and desire Catherine to collect what you will want, while my men carry to the scow such articles of furniture as will be most useful to you in your new quarters. Quick, dear Maria, I implore you, there has already been too much time lost, and I expect every moment an order from Headley to return immediately."

Sensible of a pressing emergency. Miss Heywood, with a beating heart, regained the cottage, in which so many blissful hours had been passed within the last two years, undisturbed by a care for the future, while the young officer joining his men, left one to take care of the arms of the party, and with the remainder hastened to the house making as little noise as possible, in order not to disturb the invalid. Having chosen such articles of furniture as he knew Mrs. Elmsley was most deficient in, and among these a couch and a couple of easy-chairs (which latter indeed were the work of his own hands), they were conveyed to the scow in two trips, and then followed three or four trunks into which had been thrown, without regard to order, such wearing apparel, and necessaries of the toilet as the short period allowed for preparation had permitted the agitated girl to put together. The most delicate part of the burden, however, yet remained to be removed, and that was the invalid herself. Desiring his men to remain without, the youth, whose long and close intimacy with the family rendered such a step by no means objectionable, entered the apartment of Mrs. Heywood, who had already been prepared by her daughter for the removal, and with the assistance of Catherine raised the bed on which she lay, and transferred it to a litter brought for the occasion. This they carefully bore through the suite of small and intervening rooms to the front, where two of the men relieved them, Catherine walking at the side, and unnecessarily enjoining caution at every step.

"This is, indeed, an unexpected change, Ronayne," said Miss Heywood, sadly, "but this morning, and I was so happy, and now! These poor flowers, too (for after having fastened the windows and doors of the house, they were now directing their course towards the mound), that parterre which cost us so much labor, yes, such sweet labor, must all be left to be destroyed by the hand of some ruthless savage. Yet, what do I say," she pursued, in a tone of deep sorrow, "I lament the flowers; yes, Ronayne, because they have thriven under your care, and yet, I forget that my father perhaps no longer lives; that my beloved mother's death may be the early consequence of this removal. Yet think me not selfish. Think me not ungrateful. Come what may, you will yet be left to me. No, Harry," and she looked up to him tearfully, "I shall never be utterly destitute, while you remain."

"Bless you, thrice bless you for these sweet avowals of your confidence," exclaimed the youth, suddenly dropping her arm, and straining her passionately to his heart. "Yes, Maria, I shall yet remain to love, to cherish, to make you forget every other tie in that of husband--to blend every relationship in that of one."

"Nay, Ronayne," she quickly returned, while the color mounted vividly to her cheek, under the earnest ardor of his gaze, "I would not now unsay what I have said, and yet I did not intend that my words should exactly bear that interpretation--nor is this a moment--"

"But still you will be my wife--tell me, Maria?" and he looked imploringly into her own not averted eyes. "You will be the wife, as you have long been the friend and companion of your Ronayne--answer me. Will you not?"

Her head sank upon his shoulder, and the heaving of her bosom, as she gently returned his embrace, alone conveyed the assurance he desired. She was deeply affected. She knew the ardent, generous nature of her lover, and she felt that every word that had just fallen from his lips, tended only to unravel the true emotions of his heart: but soothing as was his impassioned language, she deemed it almost criminal, at such a moment, to listen to it.

"Nay, dearest Harry," she said, gently disengaging herself from his embrace, "we will be seen. They may wonder at our delay, and send somebody back from the scow. Let us proceed."

"You are right," replied the young officer, again passing her arm through his own, while they continued their route, "excess of happiness must not cause me to commit an imprudence so great, as that of suffering another to divine the extent. Yet one word more, dear Maria! and ah! think how much depends upon your answer. WHEN shall I call you mine?"

"Oh! speak not now of that, Ronayne--consider the position of my father--my mother's health."

"It is for that very reason that I do ask it," returned the youth. "Should Heaven deprive you of the one, as it in some degree threatens you with the loss of the other, what shall so well console you as the tenderness of him who is blessed with your love?"

"Hush, Harry," and she fondly pressed his arm--"they will hear you."

They had now approached the scow, into which the men, having previously deposited the furniture and trunks, were preparing to embark the litter upon which Mrs. Heywood lay extended, with an expression of resignation and repose upon her calm features, that touched the hearts of even these rude men. Her daughter, half-reproaching herself for not having personally attended to her transport, and only consoled by the recollection of the endearing explanation with her lover, which had chanced to result from her absence, now tenderly inquired how she had borne it, and was deeply gratified to find that the change of air, and gentle exercise to which she had been subjected, had somewhat restored her. Here was one source of care partly removed, and she felt, if possible, increased affection for the youth to whose considerate attention was owing this favorable change in the condition of a parent, whom she had ever fondly loved.

It was near sunset when Ronayne, who, with the robust Catherine, had carefully lifted the invalid into the centre of the scow, reached the landing-place below the Fort. Here were collected several of the women of the company, and among them Mrs. Elmsley, who had come down to meet and welcome those for whose reception she had made every provision the hurried notice she had received would permit. The young officer had been the first to step on shore, and after he had whispered something in her ear, she for a moment communicated with the group of women--then advanced to meet Miss Heywood, whom her lover was now handing from the scow. She embraced her with a tenderness so unusually affectionate, that a vague consciousness of the true cause flashed across the mind of the anxious girl, recalling back all that inward grief of soul, which the deep emotion of an engrossing love had for a time absorbed.

In less than half-an-hour the fugitives were installed in the council hall, and in another small apartment, dividing it from the rooms occupied by the Elmsleys. The ensign, having seen that all was arranged in a suitable manner in the former, went out to the parade-ground, leaving the ladies in charge of their amiable hostess, and of the women she had summoned to assist in bearing the latter into the Fort.

On his way to his rooms, he met Captain Headley returning from an inspection of the defences. He saluted him, and was in the act of addressing him in a friendly and familiar tone, when he was checked by the sharply-uttered remark:

"So, sir, you are returned at last. It seems to me that you have been much longer absent than was necessary."

The high spirit of the youth was chafed. "Pardon me, sir," he answered haughtily, "if I contradict you. No one of the least feeling would have thought of removing such an invalid as Mrs. Heywood is, without using every care her condition required. Have you any orders for me, Captain Headley?" he concluded, in a more respectful manner, for he had become sensible, the moment after he had spoken, of his error in thus evincing asperity under the reproof of his superior.

"You are officer of the guard, I believe, Mr. Ronayne?"

"No, sir, Mr. Elmsley relieved me this morning."

At that moment the last-named officer came up, on his way to the ensign's quarters, when, the same question having been put to him, and answered in the affirmative, Captain Headley desired that the moment the fishing-party came in they should be reported to him. "And now, gentlemen," he concluded, "I expect you both to be particularly on the alert to-night. The absence of that fishing-party distresses me, and I would give much that they were back."

"Captain Headley," said the ensign, quickly and almost beseechingly, "let me pick out a dozen men from the company, and I pledge myself to restore the party before mid-day to-morrow. Nay, sir," seeing strong surprise and disapproval on the countenance of the commandant, "I am ready to forfeit my commission if I fail--"

"Are you mad, Mr. Ronayne, or do you suppose that I am mad enough to entertain such a proposition, and thus weaken my force still more? Forfeit your commission if you fail! Why, sir, you would deserve to forfeit your commission, if you even succeeded in any thing so wholly at variance with military prudence. Gentlemen, recollect what I have said--I expect you to use the utmost vigilance to-night, and, Mr. Elmsley, fail not instantly to report the fishing-boat." Thus enjoining, he passed slowly on to his quarters.

"D--n your military prudence, and d--n your pompous cold-bloodedness!" muttered the fiery ensign between his teeth--scarcely waiting until his captain was out of hearing.

"Hush," interrupted Elmsley in a whisper. "He will hear you. Ha!" he continued after a short pause, during which they moved on towards the mess-room, "you begin to find out his amiable military qualities, do you! But tell me, Ronayne, what the deuce has put this Quixotic expedition into your head? What great interest do you take in these fishermen, that you should volunteer to break your shins in the wood, this dark night, for the purpose of seeking them, and that on the very day when your ladye faire honors these walls, if I may so dignify our stockade, with her presence for the first time. Come, come, thank Headley for his refusal. When you sit down to-morrow morning, as I intend you shall, to a luxurious breakfast of tea, coffee, fried venison, and buckwheat-cakes, you will find no reason to complain of his adherence to military prudence."

"Elmsley," returned his friend, seriously, "I can have no disguise from you at such a moment. You know my regard for Maria Heywood, although you cannot divine its depth, and could I but be the means of saving her father, you can well understand the joy I should feel."

"Certainly, my dear fellow, but you know as well as myself, that there exists not the shadow of a hope of this. That scarecrow, Giles, half-witted as he is, tells too straightforward a story."

"Elmsley," persisted his friend, "there is every hope-- every reasonable expectation that he may yet survive. Maria herself first opened my eyes to the possibility, for, until then, I had thought as you do; and deeply did her words sink in my heart, when she said, reproachfully, that, instead of sending a party to escort her, it would have been far better to dispatch them to the farm, where her father might, at that moment, be sustaining a siege-- the house being strong enough to admit of a temporary defence, by even a couple of persons."

"And what said you to that?"

"What could I say? I looked like a fool, and felt like a school-boy under the iron rod of a pedagogue--but I resolved."

"And what did you resolve, my enterprising KNIGHT errant?"

"You have just heard my proposal to the gentleman who piques himself upon his military prudence." returned the youth, with bitter irony.

"Yes, and he refused you. What then?"

"True, and what then," and he nodded his head impatiently.

"You will sleep upon it, my dear fellow, after we have had a glass of the Monongahela, and the pipe. Thus refreshed, you will think better of it in the morning."

"We will have the Monongahela and the pipe, for truly I feel that I require something to soothe, if not absolutely to exhilarate me; but no sleep for me this night. Elmsley," he added, more seriously, "you will pass me out of the gate?"

"Pass you out of what?" exclaimed the other, starting from the chair on which he had thrown himself only the moment before. "What do you mean, man?"

"I mean that, as officer of the guard, you alone can pass me through after dark, and this service you must render me."

"Why! where are you going? Single-handed like Jack the Giant Killer to deliver, not a beautiful damsel from the fangs of a winged monster, but a tough old backwoodsman from the dark paws of the savage?"

"Elmsley," again urged the ensign, "you forget that Mr. Heywood is the father of my future wife."

"Ah! is it come to that at last. Well, I am right glad of it. But, my dear Ronayne," taking and cordially pressing his hand, "forgive my levity. I only sought to divert you from your purpose. What I can do for you, I will do; but tell me what it is you intend."

"Yet, Elmsley, before we enter further into the matter, do you not think that you will incur the serious displeasure of Military Prudence?"

"If he discovers that you are gone, certainly; and I cannot see how it can be otherwise; he will be in the fidgets all night, and probably ask for you; but even if not THEN, he will miss you on parade in the morning."

"And what will be the consequence to you? Answer me candidly, I entreat."

"Then, candidly, Ronayne, the captain likes me not well enough to pass lightly over such a breach of duty. The most peremptory orders have, since the arrival of this startling news, been given not to allow any one to leave the fort, and (since you wish me to be sincere) should I allow you to pass, it will go hard with my commission."

"How foolish of me not to have thought of that before! How utterly stupid to ask that which I ought to have known myself; but enough, Elmsley. I abandon the scheme altogether. You shall never incur that risk for me."

"Yet understand me," resumed the other, "if you really think that there is a hope of its proving more than a mere wild goose chase, I will cheerfully incur that risk; but on my honor, Ronayne, I myself feel convinced that nothing you can do will avail."

"Not another word on the subject," answered his friend; "here is what will banish all care, at least for the present."

His servant had just entered, and deposited on the mess-table hot and cold water, sugar, lime-juice, pipes, tobacco, and tumblers; when the two officers with Von Vottenberg who had just come in from visiting Mr. Heywood, sat down to indulge their social humors. Whilst the latter, according to custom, mixed the punch, which when made was pronounced to be his chef d'oeuvre, Elmsley amused himself with cutting up the tobacco, and filling the pipes. The ensign, taking advantage of their occupation, indulged himself in a reverie that lasted until the beverage had been declared ready.

The presence of the doctor, acting as a check upon the further allusion by the friends to the topic that had hitherto engrossed their attention, the little conversation that ensued was of a general nature, neither of them, however, cared much to contribute to it, so that the doctor found and pronounced them for that evening anything but entertaining companions. He, however, consoled himself with copious potations from the punch-bowl, and filled the room with dense clouds of smoke, that were in themselves, sufficient to produce the drowsiness that Ronayne pleaded in excuse of his taciturnity.

After his second glass, Elmsley, reminding the ensign that he expected him as well as the punch-brewer to breakfast with him in the morning at eight o'clock precisely, took his departure for the guard room, for the night.

CHAPTER VIII.

It was about seven o'clock on the morning succeeding the occurrences detailed in the preceding chapters, that Lieutenant Elmsley waited on the commanding officer, to relate that the fishing boat was at length in sight. These tidings were communicated as Captain Headley was preparing to sit down to breakfast--a refreshment, to which the fatigue of mind and body he had undergone during the night had not a little disposed him. True, however, to his character, he stayed not for the meal, but instantly arose, and taking his telescope accompanied the subaltern to the flagstaff battery, whence the best view of the river was commanded.

"Any thing to report, Mr. Elmsley; but I presume not, or it scarcely would have been necessary for me to ask the question?"

"Nothing, sir, of any consequence," replied the lieutenant after a moment's hesitation, "beyond a slight altercation that took place between a drunken Pottawattamie and the sergeant of the guard--but it was of a nature too. trivial to disturb you about."

"What was it, Mr. Elmsley?" inquired his superior, abruptly turning to him.

"The Indian who had probably been lying dead drunk during the day within the Fort, and had evidently just awakened from his sleep, was anxious to go to his encampment, but the sergeant, strictly obeying the order he had received from me, refused to open the gate, which seemed to annoy the Indian very much. At that moment I came up. I knew well of course that the order was not meant to extend rigidly to our Indian friends, the great mass of whom might be offended by the detention of one of their number, and I desired the sergeant to pass him through. Was I right, sir?"

"Perfectly, Mr. Elmsley; we must not offend those of the Indian tribes that are disposed to be friendly toward us, for no one knows how soon we may require their aid. The official advices I have received not only from Detroit but from Washington are of a nature to induce apprehension of hostilities between Great Britain and the United States; therefore, it would, as you justly observe, and just now particularly, be extremely bad policy to offend those whom it is so much our interest to conciliate. Still you ought to have reported the circumstance to me, and not acted on your own responsibility."

Lieutenant Elmsley bit his lip, and could scarcely control a movement of impatience. "I am glad, however, sir," he resumed after a pause, "that you find no fault with my conduct; I confess I had some little uneasiness on that score, for with you I felt that I had no right to assume the responsibility, but I knew that you had retired to your rooms, and I was unwilling to disturb you."

"You ought to have known, Mr. Elmsley, that where duty is concerned I can never be disturbed. However, no matter. What you did was correctly done; only in future, fail not to make your report. The slightest unauthorized step might be a false one, and that, under all the circumstances, is to be avoided."

Whatever the subaltern thought of the seeming self-sufficiency which had dictated the concluding part of the lecture of the commanding officer, he made no further observation, and both in silence pursued the remainder of their short route to the bastion.

Many of the men, dressed and accoutred for the morning parade, which usually took place at about nine o'clock, were grouped around, and anxiously watching the approach of the boat, as of something they had despaired of ever again beholding. Captain Headley drew his telescope to the proper focus, and after looking through it a few minutes--remarked--

"Thank Heaven, all is right--they are all there, although it is quite unaccountable to me how they could have been detained until this morning. And, oh! it seems they have taken a heavy draught of fish, for, although I cannot see the bottom of the boat, their feet are raised as if to prevent crushing or injuring something beneath them. But hold! there is something wrong, too. I do not see the usual number of muskets piled in the stern. How can this be, Mr. Elmsley?"

"Perhaps there is not the same number of men," suggested the lieutenant--"some of them, for causes connected with their detention, may be coming by land."

"Not at all. There are seven men. I think seven men compose the fishing party;

do they not?"

"Six men, besides the non-commissioned officer; yes, sir."

"I can make out Corporal Nixon, for he is steering and facing me, but for the others, I do not know them well enough to distinguish. Here, Mr. Elmsley, take the glass, and try what you can make of them."

The lieutenant gazed through the glass a moment, and then pronounced name after name, as the men severally came under the range of the lens. "Yes, sir, as you say, there is Corporal Nixon steering--then, with, their backs to us, and pulling, are first, Collins, then Green, then Jackson, then Weston, then Cass, and then Philips. But what they have in the bottom of the boat, for I now can see that plain enough, is not fish, sir, but a human body, and a dog crouched at its side. Yes! it is indeed the Frenchman's dog--Loup Garou."

"Well, I want to know!" exclaimed Ephraim Giles, who had ascended the bastion, and now stood amid the group of men, "I take it, that if that's Loup Garou, his master can't be far off. I never knowed them to be separate."

"Yes, sir, that is certainly a dead body," pursued the lieutenant--"somebody killed at the farm, no doubt. Have you any orders for the direction of the party, when they land, sir?" he inquired, as he handed back the glass to the captain.

"Just desire the drum to beat to parade," was the answer. "It wants only a few minutes of guard-mounting, and by the time the men have fallen in, and the roll is called, the boat will be here. Where is Mr. Ronayne?"

"I have not seen him this morning, sir, but believe that he is in his own rooms. He, however, knows the hour, and doubtless will be here presently."

"When the men have fallen in, come and report to me," said the captain, as he descended from the bastion, and proceeded to his own quarters, to eat his untasted breakfast.

The lieutenant touched his cap in assent, and then, having despatched a man with orders to the temporary drum-major, crossed over to the apartments of the ensign, anxious not only to excuse himself for not being able to receive his friend to his own breakfast, at the hour he had named, but to prepare him for the reception of the body of Mr. Heywood, which he doubted not, was that now on its way for interment at his own house.

On entering the mess-room, in which they had taken their punch, the previous evening, everything bore evidence of a late debauch. Ashes and tobacco were liberally strewed upon the table, while around the empty bowl, were, in some disorder, pipes and glasses--one of each emptied of all but the ashes and sediment--the other two only half-smoked, half-full, and standing amid a pool of wet, which had evidently been spilt by a not very steady hand. The windows were closed, so that the smoke clung to what little furniture there was in the room, and the whole scent of the place was an abominable compound of stale tobacco and strong whisky.

A loud snoring in the room on his right attracted his attention. He knew that it was Von Vottenberg's, and he entered to see what had kept him in bed until that late hour. The surgeon, only half-undressed, was fast asleep, not within, but on the outside of the bed-clothes. Somewhat disgusted at the sight, for Elmsley was comparatively abstemious, he shook him not very gently, when the doctor, opening his eyes with a start, half-rose upon his elbow. "Ha!" he exclaimed, "I know you mean to say that breakfast is waiting; I had forgotten all about it, old fellow."

"I mean nothing of the kind," was the reply, "but I recommend you to lose no time in dressing and turning out. The men are already on parade, and if Captain Headley, finding that you are absent, tends over here to inquire the cause, I would not give much for your future chances of swallowing whisky-punch within the walls of Chicago."

"Eh? what! what!" spluttered the surgeon, as he jumped up, drew on his boots, dipped his face in a basin of water, and hastily completed his toilet. In less than five minutes he was on parade.

Meanwhile, Lieutenant Elmsley, after giving this warning, had passed again through the mess-room, and knocked at Ronayne's door. But there was no answer.

"Hilloa, Ronayne," he called loudly, as he turned the handle of the latch, "are YOU in bed too?"

But no Ronayne was there. He looked at the bed--like the doctor's, it had been laid upon, but no one had been within the clothes.

What was the meaning of this? After a few moments of delay, he flew back to Von Vottenberg's room, but the latter was already gone. Retracing his steps, he met Ronayne's servant entering at the mess-room door.

"Where is your master?" he inquired. "How is it that he is not in his room--has not been in bed?"

"Not been in bed?" repeated the lad, with surprise. "Why, sir, he told me last night that he was very drowsy and should lie late; and, that he mightn't be disturbed, he desired me to sleep in one of the block-houses. I was only to wake him in time for guard-mounting, and as it wants but ten minutes to that, I am just come to call him."

"Clean out the mess-room directly--open the windows, and pat every thing in order," said the lieutenant, fearing that Captain Headley might, on hearing of the absence of the young officer, pay his quarters a visit in search of some clue to the cause. "I see it all," he mused, as he moved across the parade-ground. "He would not, generous fellow, get me into a scrape, by making me privy to his design, and to avoid the difficulty of the gate, has got over the pickets somewhere--yet, if so, he must have had a rope, and assistance of some kind, for he never could have crossed them without. Yet, where can he be gone, and what could he have expected to result from his mad scheme? Had he waited until now, he would have known by the arrival of the fishing-party with their sad charge, how utterly useless was all this risk."

"Well, Mr. Elmsley," said the captain, who now appeared at the front of his own door, fully dressed for parade, and preparing to issue forth in all the stateliness of command.

"The parade is formed, sir," remarked the lieutenant, confusedly, "but I cannot find the officer of the guard."

"Sir!" exclaimed Captain Headley.

"I cannot find Mr. Ronayne, sir--I have myself been over to his quarters, and looked into his bed-room, but it is clear that he has not been in bed all night."

"What is the meaning of all this? Send Doctor Von Vottenberg here immediately."

And lucky was it for that gentleman that the officer who now desired his attendance on the commandant had roused him from that Lethean slumber in which he had been, only a few minutes before, so luxuriously indulging.

"Doctor Von Vottenberg," commenced the captain, as soon as that official made his appearance before him; "you are quartered with Mr. Ronayne. Have you seen any thing of him last night or this morning--no evasion, nay," seeing that the doctor's brow began to be overclouded, "I mean no attempt to shield the young man by a suppression of the truth."

"I certainly saw him last night, Captain Headley, but not at a very late hour. We took a glass or two of punch, and smoked a couple of pipes together, but we both went to bed early, and for my part, I know that I slept so soundly as to have heard nothing--seen nothing, until I got up this morning."

The doctor spoke truly as to the time of their retirement to rest, for the ensign had left him early in the night, while he had found his way to his own bed, early in the morning.

"The boat is nearing the landing-place, sir," reported the sergeant of the guard, who now came up, and more immediately addressed Lieutenant Elmsley.

This information, for the moment, banished the subject under discussion. "Let the men pile their arms," ordered Captain Headley; "and when this is done, Mr. Elmsley, follow me to the landing-place."

In a few minutes both officers were there. The boat was within fifty yards, when the subaltern joined his captain; and the oarsmen, evidently desirous of doing their best in the presence of the commanding officer, were polling silently and with a vigor that soon brought it to its accustomed berth.

"What body is that, Corporal Nixon?" inquired the latter, "and how is it that you are only here this morning?"

"Sir," answered the corporal, removing one of his hands from the steer-oar, and respectfully touching his cap, "it's poor Le Noir, the Frenchman, killed by the Injins yesterday, and as for our absence, it couldn't be helped, sir; but it's a long report I have to make, and perhaps, captain, you would like to hear it more at leisure than I can tell it here."

By this time the men had landed from the boat, leaving the Canadian to be disposed of afterwards as the commanding officer might direct. The quick eye of the latter immediately detected the slight limping of Green, whose wound had become stiff from neglect, cold, and the cramped position in which he had been sitting in the boat.

"What is the matter with this man?" he inquired of the corporal. "What makes him walk so stiffly?"

"Nothing much the matter, captain," was the indifferent reply. "It's only a ball he got in his leg in the scrimmage last night."

"Ha! the first gun-shot wound that has come under my treatment during the three long years I have been stationed here. Quick, my fine fellow, take yourself to the hospital, and tell the orderly to prepare my instruments for probing."

"Scrimmage last night; what do you mean, Corporal Nixon--whom had you the scrimmage with?"

These remarks fell at the same moment from the lips of the commander and those of the surgeon, the latter rubbing his hands with delightful anticipation of the treat in store for him.

"With the Indians, captain," replied Nixon; "the Indians that attacked Mr. Heywood's farm."

"Captain Headley," interrupted the lieutenant, with unusual deference of manner, for he was anxious that no further reference should be made to the subject in presence of the invalids and women, who, attracted by the news of the arrival of the boat, had gathered around, partly from curiosity, partly for the purpose of getting their expected supply of fish, "do you not think it better to examine Corporal Nixon first, and then the others in turn?"

"Very true, Mr. Elmsley, I will examine them separately in the orderly-room to see how far their statements agree; yet one question you can answer here, corporal. You say that it is the body of Le Noir, killed by the Indians. Where is Mr. Heywood, then?"

The generous Elmsley felt faint, absolutely sick at heart on hearing this question; the very object be had in view in proposing this private examination was thereby threatened with discomfiture.

"Mr. Heywood has been carried off by the Indians," calmly replied the corporal, yet perceptibly paling as he spoke.

"Indeed! this is unfortunate. Let the men go to their barracks, and there remain until I send for them," ordered the commandant. "You, corporal, will come to me at the orderly-room, in half an hour from this. That will be sufficient time for you to clean yourself, and take your breakfast. None of your party, I presume, have had their breakfast yet?"

"No, your honor," answered Green, who seemed to fancy that his wound gave him the privilege of a little license in the presence of his chief, "not unless an old turkey, the grandfather of fifty broods, and as tough as shoe- leather, can be called a breakfast."

Captain Headley looked at the speaker sternly, but took no other notice of what he, evidently, deemed a very great liberty, than to demand how he presumed to disobey the order of the surgeon. Then desiring him to proceed forthwith to the hospital and have his leg dressed, he himself withdrew after postponing the parade to one o'clock.

"And are you sure, Nixon, that Mr. Heywood has been carried off by the Indians," asked Lieutenant Elmsley, the revulsion of whose feelings on hearing the corporal's answer to the question put by Captain Headley had been in striking contrast with what he had experienced only a moment before; "are you quite sure of this?"

The interrogatory was put, immediately after the commanding officer had retired, doubtingly, in a low tone, and apart from the rest of the men.

"I saw them carry him off myself, sir," again deliberately said the corporal. "The whole of the party saw it too."

"Enough, enough," pursued the lieutenant, in a friendly tone. "I believe you, Nixon. But another question. Were you joined last night by any one of the regiment? recollect yourself."

The corporal declaring that nothing in the shape of an American uniform had come under his notice, since he departed from the Fort the preceding evening, the officer next turned his attention to the boat.

"What are you fumbling about there, Collins?" he asked, rather sharply--"Why do you not go and join your mess?" This was said as the rest of the party were now in the act of moving off with their muskets and fishing apparatus.

"Poor fellow!" interposed the corporal, "he is not himself to-day; but I am sure, Mr. Elmsley, you will not be hard upon him, when I tell you that, but for him, there wouldn't be a man of us here of the whole party."

"Indeed!" exclaimed the lieutenant, not a little surprised at the information; "but we shall hear all about that presently; yet what is he fidgetting about at the bottom of the bow of the boat?"

"There's another body there, sir, besides Le Noir's. It's that of the poor boy at Heywood's--an Indian scalped him and left him for dead. Collins, who put a bullet into the same fellow, not an hour afterwards, found the boy by accident, while retreating from the place where we had the first scrimmage with the red devils. He was still breathing, and he took every pains to recover him, but the cold night air was too much for him, and he died in the poor fellow's arms."

"Well, this is a strange night's adventure, or rather series of adventures," remarked the lieutenant half aside to himself. "Then, I suppose," he resumed, more immediately addressing the corporal, "he has brought the body of the boy to have him interred with Le Noir?"

"Just so, sir, for he mourns him as if he had been his own child," answered Nixon, as the officer departed-- "here, Loup Garou, Loup Garou," and he whistled to the dog. "Come along, old fellow, and get some breakfast."

But Loup Garou would not stir at the call of his new master. Sorrow was the only feast in which he seemed inclined to indulge, and he continued to crouch near the body of the Canadian as impassible and motionless as if he was no longer of earth himself.

"Come along, Collins," gently urged the Virginian, approaching the boat, where the former was still feeling the bosom of the dead boy in the vain hope of finding that life was not yet extinct. "It's no use thinking about it; you have done your duty as a soldier, and as a good man, but you see he is gone, and there is no help for it. By and by, we will bury them both together; but come along now. The dog will let nobody near them."

"Dash me, corporal, if I ever felt so queer in my life!" answered Collins, in a melancholy tone, strongly in contrast with his habitual brusque gaiety; "but, as you say, it's no use. The poor lad is dead enough at last, and my only comfort now is to bury him, and sometimes look at his grave."

The half-hour given by Captain Headley to the men to clean themselves and eat their breakfasts, afforded his subaltern ample time to take his own, which had all this time been waiting. When he readied his rooms he found that he had another ordeal to go through. Mrs. Elmsley was already at the bead of the table, and pouring out the coffee, with Miss Heywood seated on her left--the latter very pale, and having evidently passed a sleepless night. As the officer entered the room, a slight flush overspread her features, for she looked as if she expected him to be accompanied by another, but when he hastily unbuckled his sword, and placed it, with his cap, on a side-table, desiring his wife to lose no time in pouring out the coffee, as he must be off again immediately, she felt, she knew not wherefore, very sick at heart, and became even paler than before. Nor was she at all re-assured by the tone of com-miseration in which, after drawing a chair to her side, and affectionately pressing her hand, he inquired after her own and her mother's health.

"Why, George," said Mrs. Elmsley, who remarked this change in her friend, and in some degree divined the cause, "where are Mr. Ronayne and the doctor? You told me last night they were to breakfast here--and see, one, two, three, four, five cups (pointing at each with her finger), I have prepared accordingly. Indeed, I scarcely think this young lady would have made her appearance at the breakfast-table, had she not expected to meet--who was it, my dear? and she turned an arch look upon her friend --"ah! I know now--Von Vottenberg."

"Nay, I have no more need of disguise from your husband than from yourself, Margaret," replied Miss Heywood, her coloring cheek in a measure contradicting her words--"it was Harry Ronayne I expected; but," she added, with a faint smile, "do not imagine I am quite so romantic as not to be able to take my breakfast, be-cause he is not present to share it; therefore if you please, I also will trouble you for a cup of coffee."

"All in good time," remarked Mrs. Elmsley. "I dare say, Ronayne is engaged in some duty which has prevented him from keeping his engagement as punctually as he could have desired. We shall certainly see him before the breakfast things are removed."

"It seems to me," said her husband, who was taking his meal with the appetite of any other than a hungry man, and even with a shade of vexation on his features, "that you all appear to be very much in the dark here. Why, Margaret, have you not heard what has occurred during the night, as well as this morning?"

"How should I have heard any thing, George?" replied Mrs. Elmsley. "I have seen no one since you went out this morning--who could have communicated news from without? Surely you ought to know that. Will you have more coffee?"

"No, thank you--I have no appetite for coffee or for any thing else. I almost wish I had not come. Dear Maria," he added, impetuously, taking Miss Heywood's hand in his own; "I know you have a noble--a courageous heart, and can bear philo-sophically what I have to tell you."

"I can bear much," was the reply, accompanied by a forced smile, that was con-tradicted by the quivering of the compressed lip; "and if I could not, I find I must begin to learn. Yet what can you have to tell me, my dear Mr. Elmsley, more than I already divine--my poor father--" and the tears started from her eyes.

"Ha! there at least, I have comfort for you--although there has been sad work at the farm--the fishing-party have come in with the bodies of poor Le Noir and the boy Wilton, but they all say that Mr. Heywood was carried off a prisoner by the Indians."

"Carried off a prisoner," repeated Miss Heywood, a sudden glow animating her pale features--"oh! Elmsley, thank you for that. There is still a hope then?"

"There is indeed a hope; but, dearest Miss Heywood, why must I heal with one hand and wound with the other. If I give comparative good news of your father, there is another who ought to be here, and whose absence at this moment is to me at once a pain and a mystery."

"You mean Harry Ronayne?" she said, hesitatingly, but without manifesting surprise.

"Where the foolish fellow has gone," he continued, "I do not know, but he has disappeared from the Fort, nor has he left the slightest clue by which he may be traced."

"Does Captain Headley know this?" she inquired, recollecting, that part of the conversation that had passed between them the preceding day, in reference to the succor that might have been afforded at the farm.

"He does. I made the report of Ronayne's absence to him personally, and the doctor was summoned to state if he had seen any thing of him. He, however, was as ignorant as a man, who had been drunk during the night, and was not yet quite sober in the morning, could well be. The captain was as much surprised as displeased, but further inquiry was delayed on the sergeant of the guard coming up and announcing the near approach of the boat containing the fishing-party."

"Tell me, dear Mr. Elmsley," said Miss Heywood, after a few moments of seeming reflection; "what is your own opinion of the matter? How do you account--or have you at all endeavored to account for Ronayne's absence?"

"I can easily understand the cause," he replied, "but confound me if I can attempt to divine the means he took to accomplish his object."

He then proceeded to relate the circumstances of his proposal to Captain Headley--the abrupt refusal he had met with--his subsequent application to himself to pass him out of the gate, and the final abandonment of his request when he found that his acquiescence would seriously compromise him, as officer of the guard.

"Noble Harry!" thought Miss Heywood--"your confusion, your vexation of yesterday, arose from not being able to follow your own generous impulses: but now I fully understand the resolve you secretly made--and all for my sake. Do not think me very romantic," she said aloud to Mr. Elmsley, "but really, Margaret, I cannot despair that all will yet, and speedily, be well. The only fear I entertain is that the strict Captain Headley may rebuke him in terms that will call up all the fire of his nature, and induce a retort that may prove a source of serious misunderstanding-- unless, indeed, the greatness of the service rendered, plead his justification."

"Now that we are on the subject, dear Miss Heywood," remarked Elmsley, "let me once for all disabuse you of an impression which I fear you entertain--or is it so? Do you think that Ronayne has had an opportunity of joining the party at the farm?"

"Certainly, I do," she answered, gravely, "or why should he have gone forth? Pray do not rob me of what little comfort, in expectation, I have left."

"That he went forth madly and single-handed for the purpose, I can believe-- nay, I am sure of it; but I grieve to add that he has not been seen there."

"This, indeed, is strange," she returned in faltering tones, and with ill-disguised emotion, for, hitherto she had been sustained by the belief that he was merely lingering behind the party, in order to satisfy himself of facts, the detail of which could not fail to be satisfactory to her ear. "How know you this?"

"I questioned Corporal Nixon, who commanded the party, and who apprised me of Mr. Heywood's having been carried off by the Indians, for I was deeply anxious, as you may presume, to know what had become of my friend--and this far less even for my own sake than for yours."

"And his answer was?" and there was deep melancholy in the question.

"That no American uniform had come under his notice during his absence from the Fort, save those of the party he commanded. These, as far as I can recollect, were his precise words."

"Mr. Elmsley," said a sentry, who now appeared at the door of the breakfast-parlor, "Captain Headley waits for you in the orderly room."

"Is Corporal Nixon there?" asked the lieutenant.

"He is, sir."

"Good, Dixon, I shall be there immediately."

"God bless you," he continued, to Miss Heywood, when the man had departed. "We shall, perhaps, elicit from him, something that will throw light upon the obscure part of this matter. Margaret, do not leave the dear girl alone, but cheer up her spirits, and make her hope for the best."

So saying, he shook her hand affectionately, pushed back his chair from the table, and resuming his cap and sword, left the friends together, promising to return as soon as the examination of the man should be concluded.

CHAPTER IX.

Mr. Heywood's history may be told in a few words. He was the son of an officer who had served in one of the American partizan corps, during the Revolution, and had been killed at the attack made by General Green upon the stronghold of Ninety-Six, in the South. At that time he was a mere youth, and found himself a few years after, and at the age of eighteen, without fortune, and wholly dependent upon his own resources. The war being soon ended, his naturally enterprising disposition, added to great physical strength, induced him to unite himself with one of the many bands of adventurers that poured into the then, wilds of Kentucky, where, within five years, and by dint of mere exertion and industry, he amassed money enough to enable him to repair to Charleston, in South Carolina, and espouse a lady of considerable landed property, with whom he had formed a partial engagement, prior to his entering on that adventurous life. The only fruit of this union was a daughter, and here, as far as fortune was concerned, they might have enjoyed every comfort in life, for Mrs. Heywood's property was principally situated in the neighborhood, but her husband was of too restless a nature to content himself with a sedentary life. He had at the outset embarked in commerce --the experience of a few years, however, convincing him that he was quite unsuited to such pursuits, he had the good sense to abandon them before his affairs could be involved. He next attempted the cultivation of the estate, but this failing to afford him the excitement he craved, he suddenly took leave of his family, and placing every thing under the control of a manager, once more obeyed the strong impulse, which urged him again to Kentucky. Here, following as a passion the occupation of his earlier years, he passed several seasons, scarcely communicating during that period, with his amiable and gentle wife, for whom, however, as well as for his daughter--now fifteen years of age, and growing rapidly into womanhood --he was by no means wanting in affection. Nor was his return home THEN purely a matter of choice. Although neither quarrelsome nor dissipated in his habits, he had had the misfortune to kill, in a duel, a young lawyer of good family who had accompanied him to Kentucky, and had consequently fled. Great exertions were made by the relatives of the deceased to have him arrested on the plea that the duel, the result of a tavern dispute, had been unfair on the part of the survivor. As there was some slight ground for this charge, the fact of Mr. Heywood's flight afforded increased presumption of his guilt, and such was the publicity given to the matter by his enemies, that the rumor soon reached Charleston, and finally, the ears of his family.

Revealing, in this extremity, his true position to his wife, Mr. Heywood declared it to be his intention either to cross the sea, or to bury himself forever in the remotest civilized portion of their own continent, leaving her however, to the undisturbed possession of the property she had brought him, which would of course descend to their child.

But Mrs. Heywood would not listen to the proposal. Although she had much to complain of, and to pain her, all recollection of the past faded from her memory, when she beheld her husband in a position of danger, and even in some degree of humiliation, for she was not ignorant that even in the eyes of people not over scrupulous, ineffaceable infamy attaches to the man, who, in a duel, aims with unfair deliberation at the life of his opponent; and anxious to satisfy herself that such a stain rested not on the father of her child, she conjured him to tell her if such really was the case. He solemnly denied the fact, although he admitted there were certain appearances against him, which, slight as they were, his enemies had sought to deepen into proofs--and in the difficulty of disproving these lay his chief embarrassment.

The tone--the manner--the whole demeanor of Mr. Heywood carried conviction with his denial, and his wife at once expressed her determination to renounce for his sake, all those local ties and associations by which she had been surrounded from childhood, and follow his fortunes, whithersoever they might lead. This, she persisted, she was the more ready and willing to do, because her daughter's education having been some months completed, under the best masters, there was now no anxiety on her account, other than what might arise from her own sense of the contemplated change.

Maria Heywood was accordingly summoned to the consultation --made acquainted with her father's position, and the necessity for his instant departure from that section of the country--and finally told that with her it rested to decide, not only whether he should go alone, but if they accompanied him, whether it should be to Europe, or to the Far West.

"Rest with me to decide!" exclaimed the warm-hearted girl as she threw herself into her mother's arms. "Oh, how good of you both thus to consult me, whose duty it is to obey. But do not think that it is any privation for me to leave this. I cannot claim the poor merit of the sacrifice. I have no enjoyment in cities. Give me the solitude of nature, books, and music, and I will live in a wigwam without regret."

"Dear enthusiast," said Mrs. Heywood, pressing her fondly to her heart; "I knew well in what spirit would be your answer. You decide then for the Far West?"

"Oh, yes, dear mamma! the Far West for me--no Europe. Give me the tall, dense forests of our own noble land! I desire no other home--long have I pictured to myself the vast lakes--the trackless woods and the boundless prairies of that region of which I have read so much, and now," she concluded, with exaltation, "my fondest wishes will be realized, and I shall pass my life in the midst of them. But, dear papa, to what particular spot do we go?"

"To Chicago, my noble girl! It is the remotest of our Western possessions, and quite a new country. There I may hope to pass unheeded, but how will you, dear Maria, endure being buried alive there, when so many advantages await you here?"

"Only figuratively, papa," she replied with a pensive smile stealing over her fine intellectual features. "Have no fear for me on that score, for depend upon it, with so much natural beauty to interest, it will be my own fault, if I suffer myself to be buried alive. What think you, dear mamma?"

"I think with you, my child," replied Mrs. Heywood, looking approvingly at her daughter, "that it is our duty, as it assuredly will be our pleasure to accompany your father wherever he may go."

It was now arranged that Mr. Heywood, furnished with a considerable sum of money in gold, should set out alone on the following night for their new destination, and make the necessary preparations for their reception, while his wife, through her agent, should endeavor to dispose of the estate. As it would require some time for this, and as the arrangements at Chicago could not well be completed within several months, it was settled that they should meet at Albany, early in the following autumn, where they should proceed to take possession of their new abode. For his better security and freedom from interruption, Mr. Heywood, while travelling, was to assume a feigned name, but his own was to be resumed immediately after his arrival at Chicago, for neither he nor his family could for a moment think of increasing the suspicion of guilt, by continuing a name that was not their own; and, finally, as a last measure of precaution, the free servants of the establishment, had, with the exception of Catharine, whom they were to take with them, been discharged, while a purchaser having fortunately been found, the slaves, with the estate, were handed over to a new master, proverbial for his kindness to that usually oppressed race. By these means they found themselves provided with funds more than adequate to all their future wants, the great bulk of the sum arising from the sale of the estate being vested in two of the most stable banks of the Union.

With the money he took with him, carefully deposited in his saddlebags, for he performed the whole of the journey on horseback, Mr. Heywood had caused the cottage already described, to be built and furnished from Detroit, in what, at that period, and so completely at the ultima thule of American civilization, was considered a style of great luxury. He had, however, shortly prior to his setting out for Albany, purchased several hundred acres of land, about two miles up the Southern branch of the Chicago, leaving instructions with Le Noir, whom he had engaged for a long term of service, to erect upon it a log building and outhouses. This he had been induced to do from that aching desire for physical exertion which had been familiar to him from boyhood, and which he felt could never be sufficiently indulged within the limited compass of the little village itself--subjected as he must be to the observation of the curious and the impertinent. He returned from Albany after a few months' absence, in the autumn of 1809, bringing with him his friends who occupied the cottage, while he himself obtained their assent that he should inhabit the farm house, completed soon after his return. Here he cut with his own hands, many a cord of the wood that his servants floated down in rafts, not only for his own family, but to supply the far more extensive wants of the garrison, with which, however, he had little or no intercourse, beyond that resulting from his business relations.

Such was the condition of things at the period at which our narrative has opened. Maria Heywood had now been three years an occupant of the cottage, and within that time solitude and habits of reflection had greatly matured her mind, as years had given every womanly grace to her person. The past had also tended much to form her character, upon which the development of physical beauty so often depends. At her first debut into society at Charleston, in her fourteenth year--an age that would have been considered premature, but for the rapidity with which form and intellect are known to ripen in that precocious climate--she had received, but listened with indifference to the vapid compliments of men whose shallowness she was not slow to detect, and whose homage conveyed rather a fulsome tribute to her mere personal beauty, than a correct appreciation of her heart and understanding. Not that it is to be inferred that she prided herself unduly upon this latter, but because it was by that standard of conduct chiefly, that she was enabled to judge of the minds of those who evinced so imperfect a knowledge of the female heart, when, emerging from the gaiety of girlhood, it passes into the earnestness of womanly feeling.

But although cold--almost repellant to all who had poured their ephemeral and seldom varying homage in her ear--no woman's heart ever beat with more kind-- more generous--more devoted sentiments, than her own. Possessed of a vivid imagination, which the general quietude of her demeanor in a great degree disowned, she had already sketched within her glowing mind her own beau ideal, whose image was a talisman to deaden her heart against the influence of these soulless realities.

With such sentiments as these had Maria Heywood cheerfully consented to accompany her parents to that secluded spot, from which there was little probability of a speedy return; but solitude, so far from weakening the strong impressions that had entwined themselves around her heart, from the moment of her emancipation from childhood, only served to invest them with new power. The more her feelings repined--the more expanded her intellect--the stronger became the sense of absence of one who could enter into, and in some degree, give a direction to all her thoughts and emotions--sharing with her the rich fruit that springs from the consciousness of kindred associations of mind. But this was the secret of her own heart--of the heart of one whose personal attractions were well suited to the rich and overflowing character of her soul, and who had now attained that age which gives eloquent expression to every movement of the ripely moulded form.

Above the middle size, the figure of Maria Heywood was at once gracefully and nobly formed. Her face, of a chiselled oval, was of a delicate olive tint, which well harmonized with eyes of a lustrous hazel, and hair of glossy raven black. A small mouth, bordered by lips of coral fulness, disclosed, when she smiled, teeth white and even; while a forehead, high for her sex, combined with a nose, somewhat more aquiline than Grecian, to give dignity to a countenance that might, otherwise, have exhibited a character of voluptuous beauty. Yet, although her features, when lighted up by vivacity or emotion, were radiant with intelligence; their expression when in repose was of a pensive cast, that, contrasted with her general appearance, gave to it a charm, addressed at once to sense and sentiment, of which it is impossible, by description, to give an adequate idea. A dimpled cheek, an arm, hand and foot, that might have served the statuary as a model, completed a person which, without exaggeration, might be deemed almost, if not wholly faultless.

The habits of Mr. Heywood were of that peculiar nature --his desire of isolation from every thing that could be called society was so obvious, that for the first year of the residence of the family at Chicago, scarcely any intercourse had been maintained between the inmates of the cottage and the officers' wives; and it was only on the occasion of the commanding officer giving a party, to celebrate the anniversary of American Independence on the following year, that the first approach to an acquaintance had been made. It had been deemed by him a matter of duty to invite all of the few American families that were settled in the neighborhood, and of course the Heywoods were of the number. On the same principle of conventionalism the invitation was accepted, and not slight was the surprise of the ladies of the garrison, when they found in the secluded occupants of the cottage, to whom they had assigned a doubtful position in society, those to whom no effort of their own prejudice could refuse that correct estimate, which quiet dignity without ostentation, is ever certain to command.

At the announcement of the names of Mrs. and Miss Heywood, the somewhat stately Mrs. Headley was disposed to receive with hauteur the inmates of the cottage, but no sooner had Maria Heywood, accompanied by her gentle mother, entered the apartment with the easy and composed air of one to whom the drawing-room is familiar, than all her prejudices vanished, and with a heart warming towards her, as though she, had been the cherished sister of her love, she arose, pressed her hand affectionately and welcomed her to the Fort with the sincerity of a generous and elevated nature, anxious to repair its own wrong.

From that period, both by the wife of the commandant, and by Mrs. Elmsley-- the only two ladies in the garrison, Maria Heywood was as much liked and courted, as she had previously been disregarded. To deny that the noble girl did in some measure exult in this change, would be to do wrong to the commendable pride of a woman, who feels that the unjust prejudice which had cast a false shadow over her recent life, has at last been removed, and that the value, of which she was modestly conscious, began to be appreciated.

It was at this party that her acquaintance with the young Southerner had commenced, and it is needless to trace the gradual rise of an attachment which similarity of tastes had engendered. Naturally of an ardent disposition, the youth had, as we have remarked on a previous occasion, hitherto loved to indulge in the excitement of the wild sports of the forest and the prairie, as the only present means of giving freedom to that spirit of enterprise, so usually wedded to the generous and unoccupied mind; but, from the period of his acquaintance with Maria Heywood, a total change had come over his manner of life. The hunt--the chase--and the cup that so often succeeded, were now almost wholly abandoned, and his only delight NOW in excursions was to ride with her across the prairie, or to pull her in his light skiff either along the shores of the Michigan, or through the various branches of the river, contemplating the beautiful Heavens by moonlight, and indulging in speculations, which were not more the fruit of romantic temperament, than of the intensity of Love. He had, moreover, four dogs trained to draw her in a light sledge of his own device and construction, in winter. In these rambles she was usually accompanied either by Mrs. Headley, or by the wife of his friend and brother subaltern, and after the invigorating exercise of the day, his evenings, whenever he could absent himself from the Fort, were devoted within the cottage to books, magic, and the far more endearing interchange of the resources of their gifted minds. In summer there were other employments of a domestic character, for in addition to their rides, walks, and excursions on the water, both found ample scope for the indulgence of their partiality for flowers, in the taste for practical horticulture possessed by Ronayne, under whose care had grown the luxuriant beauty which every where pervaded the little garden, and made it to the grateful girl a paradise in miniature.

Thus had passed nearly two years, and insensibly, without a word of love having been breathed, each felt all the security which a consciousness of being beloved alone could yield, and that assurance imparted to their manner and address when alone a confiding air, the more endearing from the silence of their lips. But although no word uttered by themselves proclaimed the existence of the secret and holy compact, not only were they fully sensible of it themselves, but it was obvious to all --even to the least observant of the garrison, and many were there, both among the soldiers and their wives--by all of whom the young ensign was liked for his openness and manliness of character--who expressed a fervent hope that the beautiful and amiable Miss Heywood would soon become the bride of their favorite officer. This it was, which had led the men of the fishing-party to express in their way, their sorrow for the young lady, when she should hear of the events at the farm-house, even while passing their rude encomiums on the sweetness of disposition of her, whom they already regarded as the wife of their young officer.

It was nearly noon, and Lieutenant Elmsley had not yet made his appearance with the promised report. Maria Heywood had, after passing an hour with her mother, returned to the breakfast-room, which it will be recollected opened immediately upon the barrack-square. Her friend being engaged with her domestic affairs, which every lady was at that period in a measure compelled to superintend, she had thrown herself (still in her morning dishabille) on a couch with a book in her hand, but with a mind wholly distracted from the subject of its pages. After continuing some time thus, a prey to nervous anxiety, as much the result of Elmsley's long absence as of her former fears, the sound of the fifes and drums fell startlingly, she knew not wherefore, upon her ear and drew her to the door. The men were falling in, and in the course of a few minutes the little line was formed a few yards to her left, with its flanks resting on either range of building, so that the mess-room door, then open, was distinctly visible in front. At the same moment, Captain Headley and the lieutenant, followed by Corporal Nixon and the other men of the fishing-party-- Green only excepted--passed out of the orderly room on her right, moved across, and took up their position in front of the parade.

"God bless me, Maria, what is that, or is it his ghost!" suddenly and unguardedly exclaimed Mrs. Elmsley, who had that moment joined her friend--placing her arm at the same time round her waist.

"What do you mean, Mar--" but before Maria Heywood could complete her sentence, all power of speech was taken from her in the emotion with which she regarded what, after a momentary glance, met her view.

It was her lover, fully equipped for parade, and walking towards the men with a calm and deliberate step, which seemed to evince total unconsciousness that any thing unusual had happened.

"Here is a chair, my love--you really tremble as if the man was a ghost. Now then, we shall have a scene between him and our amiable commandant."

"God forbid!" tremulously answered the almost bewildered girl; "I am the cause of all."

"You! Stuff, Maria. What nonsense you talk, for a sensible girl. How should you be the cause? but, positively, Ronayne can never have been away from the Fort."

"Do you think so, Margaret?"

"I am sure of it. Only look at him. He is as spruce as if he had only just come out of a band-box. But hush, not a word. There, that's a dear. Lean your head against my shoulder. Don Bombastes speaks!"

"No sign of Mr. Ronayne yet?" demanded Captain Headley, his back turned to the slowly advancing officer, whose proximity not one of the men seemed inclined to announce, possibly because they feared rebuke for insubordination. Mr. Elmsley, he pursued to that officer, who, acting on a significant half-glance from his friend, was silent also as to his approach. "Let a formal report of his absence without leave, be made to me immediately after the parade has been dismissed."

"Nay, sir," said the ensign, in his ordinary voice and close in the ear of the speaker, "not as having been absent from duty, I trust. I am not aware that I have ever missed a guard or a parade yet, without your leave."

At the first sound of his voice, the surprised commandant had turned quickly round, and there encountered the usual deferential salute of his subordinate.

"But, Mr. Ronayne, what means this? Where, sir, have you been? and, if not absent, why thus late? Do you know that the men have already been paraded, and that when required for your guard, you were not to be found?"

"The fatigues of the night, Captain Headley," returned the young officer, with some hesitation of manner; "the incessant watching--surely there--"

"I knew he had not been out of the Fort. Courage, Maria! was audible to the men who were nearest to the speaker, from Elmsley's doorway.

"I know what you would urge, Mr. Ronayne," remarked the captain; you would offer this in plea for your late appearance. I make all due allowance in the matter; but, let me tell you, sir, that an officer who thoroughly understands his duty, and consults the interests of the service, would make light of these matters, in cases of strong emergency."

"Poor Ronayne!" sighed Maria, to her friend. "This is terrible to his proud spirit. In presence of the whole of the men, too!"

"I told you, my dear, there would be a row, but never fear--Elmsley be there. See, he is looking significantly at us, as if to call our attention to what is passing."

The lieutenant had been no less astonished than the captain, at the unexpected appearance of Ronayne--even more so, indeed--because he had observed, without, however, remarking on it, the cool and unhastened pace at which he moved along the square, from the direction of the mess-room. "Now it is coming," he thought, and half- murmured to himself, as he saw the crimson gathering on his brow, during the last harsh address of his superior.

"Captain Headley," said the young man, drawing himself up to his full height, and somewhat elevating his voice, for be had remarked there were other and dearer eyes upon him, than those immediately around. "I WILL NOT be spoken to in this manner, before the men. If you think I have been guilty of a breach of duty or of discipline, I am prepared to meet your charges before the proper tribunal, but you shall not take the liberty of thus addressing me in public parade. My sword, sir," and he unbuckled it, and offered the handle, "is at, your disposal, but I deny your further right."

"No, no, no!" shouted several men from the ranks

"No. no, no!" repeated almost every man of the fishing- party, in even more energetic tones, while the commanding officer was glancing his eye keenly and rapidly along the little line, to detect those who had set the example of insubordination.

"Ugh! wah! good soger!" came from one of a small party of Indians in the rear, as the disconcerted captain turned, frowningly, from the men in front to those who had followed him from the orderly room, and now stood grouped on the inner flank.

"What is the meaning of all this?" he cried, in a loud and angry voice.

"Am I braved in my own command, and by my own men? Mr. Elmsley, who are these Indians, and how came they in?"

"They are a part of the encampment without, sir. There was no order given against their admission this morning, besides it is Winnebeg, and you have said that the gates of the Fort was to be open to him at all hours."

"Ah! Winnebeg, my friend, how do you do. I did not know it was you or your people. You know you are always welcome."

"How do, gubbernor," answered the chief, coming round from the rear of the line, and taking the proffered hand--"'Spose not very angry now--him good warrior--him good soger," and he pointed to the young subaltern.

"Ensign Ronayne is, no doubt, very sensible to your good opinion," remarked the captain, with evident pique; "but, Winnebeg, as I am sure you never allow a white man to interfere with you, when you find fault with your young chiefs, you must let me do the same."

"What find him fault for?" asked the chief, with some surprise; "brave like a devil!"

"Captain Headley," interposed the ensign, with some impatience, "am I to surrender my sword, or resume my duty?"

But the captain either could not, or would not give a direct answer. "Can you give me a good reason, Mr. Ronayne, why I should not receive your sword? Do you deny that you have been guilty of neglect of duty?"

"In what?" was the brief demand.

"In being absent from the Fort, without leave, sir."

"Indeed! To substantiate that, you must bring proofs, Captain Headley. Who," and he looked around him, as if challenging his accuser, "pretends to have seen me beyond these defences?"

The commandant was for some moments at a loss, for he had not anticipated this difficulty. At length he resumed. "Was it not to be absent without leave, that, when the guard was all ready to be marched off, you were not to be found?"

"Had the guard been marched off, or the parade even formed, I should of course, have come justly under your censure, Captain Headley; but it was not so--you ordered the parade and guard-mounting for a later hour. I am here at that hour."

"Hem!" returned the commandant, who was in some degree obliged to admit the justice of the remark; "you defend yourself more in the spirit of a lawyer, than of a soldier, Mr. Ronayne, but all this difficulty is soon set at rest. I require but your simple denial that you have been absent from the Fort, within the last twenty-four hours. That given, I shall be satisfied."

"And that, sir," was the firm reply of the youth, "I am not disposed to give. I am not much versed in military prudence, Captain Headley," he pursued, after a few moments' pause, and in a tone of slight irony, which that officer did not seem to perceive, "but at least sufficient to induce me to reserve what I have to say for my defence. You have charged me, sir, with having been absent from the Fort without leave; and it is for you to prove that fact before a competent authority."

"March off your guard, Mr. Ronayne," was the abrupt rejoinder of the commandant, for he liked not the continuation of a scene in which the advantage seemed not to rest with him, but with the very party whom he had sought to chasten; "Mr. Elmsley dismiss the parade. I had intended promoting on the spot, Corporal Nixon and private Collins for their conduct yesterday, but the gross insubordination I have just seen, has caused me to change my mind. Neither shall have the rank intended, until the guilty parties are named. I give until the hour of parade to-morrow for their production, and if, by that time, their names are not laid before me, no such promotion shall take place while I command the garrison. Dismiss the men, sir. Here, Winnebeg, my good fellow, you have come at a good moment. I have dispatches to send to Detroit this very evening, and I know no one I can trust so well as yourself."

"Good," was the answer, "Winnebeg always ready to do him order--no angry more, gubbernor, with young chief," pointing to the ensign, as he moved off with his small guard. "Dam good soger--you see dis?" and he touched his scalping-knife with his left hand, and looked very significantly.

"No, Winnebeg, not angry any more," was the reply; "but how do you know him to be good soger? What has your scalping-knife to do with it?"

"Winnebeg know all," said the chief gravely, as he laid his heavy hand upon the shoulder of the commandant, "but can't tell. Young chief say no, and Winnebeg love young chief."

This remark forcibly struck Captain Headley, and brought back to his mind, certain recollections. He, however, asked no further question, but pointed, as they moved in the direction of his own apartments, towards the sun, showing by his gesture that it was not too early to take the mid-day dram.

"Where the devil have you been, man, and with what confounded impudence you got through the scrape," was remarked at a distant part of the same ground, and at the same moment with the conversation just given.

"How is Maria?" eagerly asked Ronayne. "When shall I see her?"

"Well enough to hear all that passed between you and Military Prudence," returned his friend; "but that is no answer to my question."

"There was nothing like braving it," answered the other evasively; "but I say, Elmsley, I am devilish hungry, that breakfast you invited me to last night is over long ago, of course." This last sentence was uttered in a mock piteous tone.

"Just what I was going to speak about, my dear boy. We have had number ONE, but before half an hour, we shall be seated at number TWO. When your sergeant has relieved his sentries, come over and you will find a piping hot breakfast."

"Will it be quite consistent with military prudence to leave my guard so soon, after the lecture I have had?" remarked the ensign, with a smile--"but, ah! I had nearly forgotten. Elmsley, I must say a few words to you before I go in, and a better opportunity cannot be afforded than while we are walking from this to your place. Just go then, and order the breakfast as you propose, and return here. I shall have completed the arrangements of the guard by that time, and all that I have to ask of you, can be answered as we go along."

"I hope it is no great secret you have to impart," returned the lieutenant, "for I am a sad hand at the mysterious, and shall be sure to tell my wife, if I do not tell Maria."

"Not you--you will tell neither, but au revoir."

CHAPTER X.

At the moment when Ensign Ronayne removed his sword, with the intention of handing it to his commanding officer, in anticipation of the arrest which he expected, Maria Heywood, little conversant with those military formalities, and apprehending from the previous high tone of her lover, that something fearful was about to occur, had not absolutely fainted, but become so agitated, that Mrs. Elmsley was induced to take her back to the sofa, on which she had previously been reclining. As she was leaving her chair, Mrs. Headley, whose attention had also been arrested by the loud and angry voice of her husband, came from her own door and joined the little group, anxiously inquiring the cause of the disturbance without.

In a few brief sentences, and as correctly as she was able, Mrs. Elmsley explained to her the circumstances, and although her attentive auditor offered no very pointed remark, it was evident from her manner that she deeply deplored that strict military punctilio, which had led the husband whom she both loved and esteemed, to place himself in a false position with his own force--for that it was a false position in some degree, to provoke insubordination, and yet be without the power to punish it, she had too much good sense not to perceive. She felt the more annoyed, because she had on more than one occasion, observed that there was not that unanimity between her husband and Lieutenant Elmsley, which she conceived ought to exist between parties so circumstanced --a commander of a remote post, and his second in command, on whose mutual good understanding, not only the personal security of all might depend, but the existence of those social relations, without which, their isolated position involved all the unpleasantness of a voluntary banishment. This had ever been to her a source of regret, and she had on several occasions, although in the most delicate and unobtrusive manner, hinted at the fact; but the man who doated upon her, and to whom, in all other respects, her desire was law, evinced so much inflexibility in all that appertained to military etiquette, that she had never ventured to carry her allusions beyond the light commentary induced by casual reference to the subject.

If then she lamented that unfortunate coolness, if not absolute estrangement, which existed between Lieutenant Elmsley and her husband, bow much more acutely did she feel the difficulty of the position now, when the only other responsible officer of the garrison--and that a young man of high feeling and accomplishment, whom she had ever liked and admired--was fast being led into the same antagonism. Nay, what rendered the matter more painful to her, was the fact of the latter being the lover, or perhaps the affianced of a girl, whom she regarded with a fervor not often felt by one woman for another, and for whose interests she could have made every sacrifice, not affecting those of her husband.

Such were the women who were now seated on the ottoman, engaged more in their own reflections, than in conversation, when Lieutenant Elmsley entered the room, announcing that the truant would shortly be in for breakfast, which, he requested, might be instantly prepared in the usual manner, only adding thereto a couple of bottles of claret.

"Ah! pardon me, Mrs. Headley," he added, somewhat stiffly, as his wife left the room to issue the necessary orders, "I did not see you, or I should have been rather more ceremonious in my domestic communications."

Mrs. Headley slightly colored. She was sensible that pique towards her husband, and a belief that she wholly shared his sentiments, had induced this rather sarcastic speech.

"By no means, Mr. Elmsley. I trust you will not put ME down as a stranger, whatever your disposition to others."

There was a significance in the manner in which this was said, that deeply touched the lieutenant, and his tone immediately changed.

"Then, I take you at your word," he said. "It is a long time since I have had the pleasure of seeing you here, and you must positively join our second breakfast. I know Captain Headley is engaged with Winnebeg, whom he purposes sending off this evening with despatches, so that you will not be missed for at least an hour. There, look at Miss Heywood's imploring look--she pleads with her eyes in my favor, although there is no chance, it appears, of getting a word from her lips."

"Nay," remarked the other, who had rallied from her late despondency, on hearing the object of the breakfast; "you are very unreasonable, Mr. Elmsley. You do not deserve that I should speak to you to-day, and I am not quite sure that I shall."

"And pray, fair lady, why not? Wherein have I had the misfortune to offend?"

"Ah! do you forget? You promised to bring me a certain report of certain occurrences, and yet instead of that, not a word have you condescended to address to me until this moment."

"I plead guilty," he answered deprecatingly, "but pray for a suspension of sentence, until the return of one through whose influence I hope to obtain your pardon! I go now," he whispered, "to lead him to your feet."

"Well, what is the great question you have to put to me?" said the lieutenant to his friend, whom he had rejoined, and with whom he now returned slowly towards the house--"one involving a case of life and death it might be imagined, from the long face you put on when alluding to the matter."

"Nay, not exactly that, but still involving a good deal. Tell me frankly, Elmsley, has Miss Heywood heard any further account of the events at the farm-house?"

"She has heard the report brought in by Nixon and the rest of the fishing-party."

"And what was that, I pray you?" eagerly returned the ensign.

"That Mr. Heywood had been carried off by the Indians."

"From whom did she hear it?"

"It was I who told her, on the strength of what the corporal reported, not only to myself, but to Captain Headley."

"You are a considerate fellow, Elmsley," said his friend, warmly pressing his hand. "I thank you for that, and now that the great question, as you term it, is answered, I am quite ready for the promised breakfast. Did these fellows bring home any fish? I have a great fancy for fish this morning."

"No; they brought home dead men," and the lieutenant looked searchingly into the face of his companion, dwelling on every word, moreover, as if he would convey that he (Ronayne), knew perfectly well what freight the boat had brought to the Fort.

Further remark was prevented by their arrival at their destination--the front-door being open, and revealing the little party within. The first upon, whom the young officer's eye fell, was Mrs. Headley, of whose intended presence, his friend had not thought of apprising him. Still smarting under a keen sense of the severity of reproof of his commanding officer, and falling into the common error of involving the wife in the unamiability of the husband, Ronayne would have retired, even at the risk of losing his breakfast, and, what was of far more moment to him, of delaying his meeting with her to whom his every thought was devoted. But when Mrs. Headley, who had remarked the movement, came forward to the door, and gave him her hand with all the warmth and candor of her noble nature, the pique vanished from his mind, and in an instant, he, like Elmsley, evinced that devotion and regard for her, which her fascinating manner could not fail to inspire.

The sense of constraint being thus banished by the only one whose presence had occasioned it, the party, after a few minutes low conversation between the lovers, sat down gaily to a meal--half-break fast, half-luncheon, at which the most conspicuous actor was the lately reprimanded ensign.

"Really, Mr. Ronayne, you must have met with a perfect chapter of adventures during your absence last night. You have devoured the last four fresh eggs, my cook says, there were in the house--three limbs of a prairie fowl, and nearly the half of a young bear ham. Do, pray, tell us where you have been to gain such an appetite? Indeed you must--I am dying to know."

"My dear Mrs. Elmsley," he replied, coloring, "where should I have been but in the Fort?"

"True! where SHOULD you have been, indeed; but this is not the point, my hungry gentleman. Where WERE you? If I was, I KNOW WHO," she added, significantly, "I should have my suspicions, unless, indeed, you have already confessed within the few minutes you have been in the room."

"Nay, do not imagine I have so much influence over the truant, as to compel him to the confessional," said Maria Heywood. "I assure you I am quite as much in the dark as any one present."

"Come, Mr. Ronayne, recount your adventures," added Mrs. Headley. "Recollect you are not on parade now, or exactly before the sternest Court of Inquiry in the world, and should therefore, entertain no dread of punishment on your self-conviction."

"Thus urged and encouraged," said the ensign, during one of the short pauses of his knife and fork, which, in truth, he had handled as much to study what he should say, as to satisfy his hunger; "who could resist such pleading, were there really any thing to communicate; but I am quite at a loss to conceive why so general an opinion seems to prevail that I have been out of the Fort, and in quest of adventure. Why not rather ascribe my tardiness at parade to some less flattering cause--a head-ache--fatigue from night-watching--indolence, or even a little entetement, arising from the denial of a very imprudent request I made to Captain Headley last evening, to allow me the command of a detachment for a particular purpose. Pardon me, I have made quite a speech, but indeed you compel me."

"Let us drown this inquisition in a bumper of claret," interposed Elmsley, coming to the assistance of his friend, whose motive for thus parrying inquiry into his conduct, he thought he could divine. "I say, my dear fellow, you may wish yourself a head-ache--fatigue-- indolence, or even a little entetement every morning of your life, if it is to be cured in this manner. This is some of the most splendid Lafayette that ever found its way into these western wilds. Look well at it. It is of the clearest, the purest blood of the grape--taste it again. A bottle of it will do you no harm if you had twenty guards in charge."

As he had desired and expected, the introduction of his remarks on the wine proved not only a means of changing the conversation, but of causing the ladies to withdraw from the table, round which they had been sitting, rather to keep the young officer company, than to participate in the repast themselves. Mrs. Headley was the first to move.

"Give me your arm, and see me home," she said carelessly, to Ronayne, who now having finished his breakfast, had also risen. "Do not be jealous, my dear Miss Heywood, but you will later know, if you do not know already, that the wife of the commanding officer always appropriates to herself, the handsomest unmarried young officer of the regiment."

Both Ronayne and his betrothed were too quick of apprehension not to perceive, under this light gaiety, a deep interest, and a desire to convey to them both, that, if unhappily, there did not exist a cordial understanding between her husband and the former, in matters purely military, and in relation to subjects which should have no influence over private life, she was by no means, a party to the disunion.

"Not very difficult to choose between the handsomest and the cleverest of the unmarried officers of the garrison of Chicago," replied Maria Heywood with an effort at cheerfulness; "therefore, Mr. Ronayne, I advise you not to be too much elated by Mrs. Headley's compliment. After that caution, I think you may be trusted with her."

"What a noble creature, and what a pity she has so cold and pompous a husband," remarked Lieutenant Elmsley, as Mrs. Headley disappeared from the doorway. "I never knew her so well as this morning, and upon my word, Margaret, were both HE and YOU out of the way, I should be greatly tempted to fall in love with her."

"You would act wisely if you did, George; I have always thought most highly of her. She is, it is true, a little reserved in manner, but that I am sure comes wholly from a certain restraint, imposed upon her by her husband's formality of character. I say I am sure of this, for there have been occasions when I have seen her exhibit a warmth of address, as different from her general demeanor, as light is from shadow."

"Perhaps Headley has systematically drilled her into the particular bearing that ought to be assumed by the wife of the commandant of a garrison."

"Nay, George! that is not generous, but I know you are not serious in what you say. You judge Mrs. Headley better, and that she is not a woman to be so drilled. She has too much good sense, despite all her partiality for her husband, to allow herself to be improperly influenced, where her judgment condemns; and although, as his wife, she must necessarily act in concert with him, it by no means follows that she approves unreservedly, all that he does."

"You are a dear, noble creature yourself!" exclaimed the gratified Elmsley, as he fondly embraced his wife. "There is nothing I love so much as to see one woman warm in the defence of another--one so seldom meets with that sort of thing. What, Maria, tears?"

"Yes--tears of pleasure!" she answered earnestly, as she held her handkerchief to her eyes--"tears of joy to see so much generosity of feeling among those whom I have so much reason to esteem and admire. You are right," she pursued, addressing Mrs. Elmsley, "she is indeed a noble woman. Perhaps I may justly be accused of a little partiality, for I never can forget the frank and cordial proffers of friendship with which she received me on the first night of my appearance here."

"Ha! Von Vottenberg to the rescue!" exclaimed Elmsley, with sudden animation, as the stout figure of the former shaded the door-way. "Well, doctor, have you passed away in the evaporation produced by fright, the violent head-ache you were suffering from this morning? If not, try that claret. It is capital stuff, and a tumbler of it will make up for the breakfast you have lost."

"Faith, and there is no breakfast lost, that I can perceive," chuckled the doctor, seating himself unceremoniously at the table, and commencing upon the remains of the bear ham, and prairie hen.

"I fear the tea and coffee are cold," said Mrs. Elmsley; "let me get some hot for you?"

"By no means, my dear Mrs. Elmsley, I could not think of such slops with generous claret at my elbow. Nay, do not look offended. Your tea and coffee are always of the best, but they do not just now, suit my taste. Miss Heywood, how do you do this morning? How is your gentle mother? I have called expressly to see her. Elmsley, where is that runaway, Ronayne?"

And where indeed was he? They had not walked more than three or four paces, when Mrs. Headley, after some little hesitation, addressed him thus:--

"Mr. Ronayne, notwithstanding your evident desire to conceal the fact, I can plainly see that you were not within the Fort last night. I can fully comprehend that your motive for absenting yourself, has been praiseworthy, but you must also admit that the reproof you met with this morning, was not altogether undeserved. Pray do not start or look grave, for, believe me, I am speaking to you only as a friend-- indeed it was to have the opportunity of convincing you that I am such, that I asked you to escort me."

"Really, Mrs. Headley," interrupted the young officer, little divining to what all this was to tend, and feeling not altogether at his ease, from the abruptness with which the subject had been introduced, "I feel as I ought, the interest you profess to take in me, but how is that connected either with my asserted absence, or the reproof it entailed?"

"It is so far connected with it, that I wish to point out the means by which any unpleasant result may be avoided!"

"Unpleasant result! Mrs. Headley?"

"Yes, unpleasant result, for I have too good an opinion of you not to believe that any thing tending to destroy the harmony of our very limited society, would be considered such by you."

"I am all attention, Madam. Pray, proceed."

"The pithiness of your manner does not afford me much encouragement yet I will not be diverted from my purpose, even by that. You have had the Commandant's lecture," she continued, with an attempt at pleasantry, "and now you must prepare yourself for (pardon the coinage of the term) that of the Commandantess."

"The plot thickens," said the ensign, somewhat sharply-- "both the husband and the wife. Jupiter Tonans and Juno the Superb in judgment upon poor me in succession. Ah! that is too bad. But seriously, Mrs. Headley, I shall receive with all due humility, whatever castigation you may choose to inflict."

"No castigation I assure you, Ronayne, but wholesome advice from one, who, recollect, is nearly old enough to be your mother. However, you shall hear and then decide for yourself."

"Although," she pursued, after a short pause, "we women are supposed to know nothing of those matters, it would be difficult, in a small place like this, to be ignorant of what is going on. Hence it is that I have long since remarked, with pain and sorrow, the little animosity which exists between Headley and yourself--(I will not introduce Mr. Elmsley's name, because what I have to say has no immediate reference to him), and the almost daily widening breach. Now, Ronayne, I would appeal to your reason. Place yourself for a moment in my husband's position. Consider his years, nearly double your own--his great responsibility and the peculiar school of discipline in which he has been brought up. Place yourself, I repeat, in his position, and decide what would be your sentiments if, in the conscientious discharge of your duty, you thought yourself thwarted by those very men--much your juniors both in years and military experience--on whose co-operation you had every fair reason to rely."

"You have, my dear Mrs. Headley, put the case forcibly yet simply." returned the ensign, who had listened with marked deference to the whole of her remonstrance. "In such a case I should feel no slight annoyance, but why imagine that I have sought to thwart Captain Headley?"

"Was it not apparently to thwart him--bear in mind I speak to you dispassionately and as a friend--to refuse in the presence of the whole garrison this morning to account for your absence of last night, which might have been easily explained, had you been so disposed?"

"But, my dear Mrs. Headley, why is it persisted in, that I was absent--and even if such were the case, might not I have had a good reason for refusing to commit myself by the avowal."

"Admitting this, could you have maintained your position without, in a measure, setting his authority at defiance --thus encouraging the men to do the same. Was this right, I ask? Was this officer-like?"

"Well, no, perhaps not. I blush not to make the admission to YOU, for indeed, there is no resisting so bewitching a master in petticoats. Yet, what would you have me do?"

"Ah, now, I begin to entertain some hope of you," she replied, in a gayer tone, placing her hand at the same time familiarly on his shoulder and looking approvingly in his face. "Ronayne, you are engaged--perhaps will shortly become the husband of the noble girl, whom I love even as though she were my own daughter--yes," she repeated energetically, as she felt his grateful pressure of her hand, "even as though she were my own daughter--nay, you know I like yourself for your open, although rather too impetuous character. Do you then think that feeling this it can be any other than a source of deep pain and vexation to me, to see those in whom I feel so much interest, alienated from each other--in some degree even mutually hating and hated?"

"Yet, what would you have me to do, my dear Mrs. Headley? Some concession I suppose, must be made. Any thing in honor and in reason will I do for your sake," returned the young officer, deeply touched by her manner and language.

"This I wish you to do, Ronayne. Take the first favorable opportunity, either while on guard to-day, or when relieved to-morrow, to see Headley privately, and by such language as you well know how to use, remove the unfavorable impression you have left on his mind--depend upon it, although extremely cold and inflexible when apparently braved, my husband has a warm and generous--aye, a noble heart, and will freely grant what is frankly solicited. Bear in mind, moreover, Ronayne, that it is no humiliation to admit error when conscious of having committed it; and if this be so in the social relations of life, how much less derogatory is it in a military sense."

"Say no more, dearest Mrs. Headley, since it is your wish, I will go, no matter what the reception I encounter; and any further rebuke I may meet with, I will cheerfully endure for your sake."

"Now then, Ronayne, you are once more yourself, the generous, high-minded boy, in whom I delighted, even as a mother would delight in her son, when you first arrived here about three years ago. Yet, recollect that not only *I* shall be gratified and benefitted by this, but YOU and YOURS. Let but this unhappy discord terminate, and we shall then be what soldiers and those connected with them, ought ever to be--one undivided family. And now, for the present, farewell."

"God bless you!" fervently exclaimed the ensign, as he took his leave of the graceful and noble wife of the commanding officer, with emotions that fully testified the effect produced upon him by her generous confidence and candor.

From the frequent reference made by Mrs. Headley to her own riper years, one might have been induced to consider her rather in the decline of life; but such was not the case. Her splendid and matronly figure might indeed have impressed the superficial observer with the belief that she had numbered more than forty summers, but the unchained and luxuriant hair--the white, even and perfect teeth-- the rich, full lip, and unwrinkled brow, and smooth and brilliant cheek, would not have permitted the woman most jealous of her charms, could such have been found, to pronounce her more than six-and-thirty, which was, indeed, her age. It was a source of gratification to her to consider and represent herself as older than she really was; and if she had any peculiarity--a weakness it could not be called--it was that of loving to look upon those younger persons who claimed a place in her friendship and esteem, as though she actually stood in the maternal relation to them. This may have, in some degree, arisen from the fact of her having ever been childless herself.

As Ronayne approached Elmsley's house on his return, a remarkably handsome and noble-looking Indian--quite a youth--was leaning against the frame of the door, and according to the simple habit of his race, indulging his curiosity by looking at, and admiring all that he beheld within. Elmsley himself had gone out, but Von Vottenberg, still seated at the breakfast-table, was discussing, with its remains, the now nearly finished claret, while Mrs. Elmsley and Maria Heywood were seated on the sofa opposite to the door, passing their whispered remarks on the Indian, whose softened dark glances occasionally fell with intense admiration on the former, when he fancied the act unseen, but as instantly were withdrawn, when he perceived that it was observed.

Mrs. Elmsley was endeavoring to dissipate the dejection of her friend by rallying her, as the young officer came to the door, on the evidently new conquest she had made. The Indian turned to look at the intruder upon his pleasant musings, when a "wah!" expressive of deep satisfaction escaped him, and at the same moment, Ronayne grasped, and cordially shook his hand.

"Ha! there is his formidable rival, and seemingly his friend," whispered Mrs. Elmsley, in the ear of Maria-- "handsome fellows, both of them, so much so, that were I single, like you, I should have some difficulty in choosing between them."

As she uttered these words, a sharp and unaccountable pang, sudden and fleeting as electricity, shot through the frame of her friend. The blood suddenly receded from her cheek, and then rapidly returning, suffused it with a burning heat.

"What is the matter, my love? Are you ill, you looked so pale just now?" tenderly inquired Mrs. Elmsley.

"I cannot account for what I experienced. It was a feeling different from any I had ever known before--a strange, wild, and inexplicable dread of I know not what. But it has passed away. Take no notice of it, dear, before Ronayne."

"Mrs. Elmsley," said the latter, almost using force to induce the modest-looking young Indian to enter the room, "will you allow me first to introduce my friend Waunangee to you, and then to give him a glass of claret? Forgive the liberty I take, but I confess a good deal of obligation to him, and would fain do the civil in return."

"Indeed! what a set speech for a glass of wine. Give it to him by all means, if it is only for his beautiful eyes--that is to say, if the doctor has left any--or stay, I will get another bottle."

"By no means," returned the young officer, "this unconscionable man has just left about half a tumbler foil, and I do not intend he shall have more. Waunangee," he pursued, after filling and presenting him with the glass, "that is the lady of the house," pointing to Mrs. Elmsley, "you must drink to her health."

"And dis you handsome squaw," remarked the Indian, a moment or two after having tossed off the wine, which quickly circulated through his veins. "Dis you wife!" he repeated, throwing his expressive eyes upon Miss Heywood, while a rich glow lighted up his dark, but finely formed features.

"Hush!" said Ronayne, making a sign to intimate that he was not to indulge in such observations.

But even the small quantity of wine he had taken was acting potently on the fast animating Indian. "Dis no you squaw--dis Waunangee squaw," he said, with strong excitement of manner. "Waunangee, see him beautiful, Waunangee got warm heart--love him very much!"

"Tolerably well for a modest youth!" exclaimed the laughing Mrs. Elmsley. "Who would have thought that one with those soft black eyes, more fitted for a woman than a man, would hazard so glowing a speech, after an acquaintance of barely five minutes?"

"Who says Chicago doesn't abound in adventure?" sneered Von Vottenberg, as he arose and passed into the apartment of his patient. "I shall certainly write a book about this when I get back into the civilized world, and entitle it 'The Loves of the Handsome Waunangee, and the Beautiful American.'"

"You had better write 'The Loves of the Fat Von Vottenberg, and his Mistress, Whisky Punch,'" remarked Ronayne, peevishly, for in spite of himself, he felt annoyed at an observation, which he thought delicacy might have spared. "Come, Waunangee, my good friend, we must go."

But the young Indian was not so easily led. "Waunangee have him first dis nice squaw," he said, with all that show of dogged obstinacy which so usually distinguishes his race, when under the influence of liquor, and bent upon the attainment of a particular object.

"Hear me, Waunangee," replied the other, placing his hand upon his shoulder, and now, that Mrs. Elmsley only was present with his affianced, feeling less scruple in explaining to the young savage--"that is my squaw--my wife."

"Why you no tell him so?" asked the youth, gravely, and with an air of reproach, while, at the same time, he fixed his soft and melancholy eyes upon Miss Heywood. "Waunangee love officer's squaw--but Waunangee good heart. Shake him hand, my friend," he continued, walking up to her, and tendering his own, while, singular as it seemed to all, a tear dimmed his eye, and stole down his cheek. "'Spose no Waunangee wife--you Waunangee's friend?"

The generous but trembling girl, shook cordially the hand that rested in her own, and assured the youth, in a way easily intelligible to him, that, as the friend of her husband, and she blushed deeply, as the moment afterwards she became sensible she had used a word, she could not but feel to be premature, she would always regard him with friendship and esteem.

"What a nice little scene we might get up out of this morning's adventure," said the ever gay Mrs. Elmsley, as Waunangee, after having shaken hands with herself, departed with Ronayne. "Really, my dear, he is a fine looking, and certainly a warm-hearted fellow, that Wau--Wan--what's his name, Maria?"

"Waunangee. I know not how it is, Margaret, or why--I should attach so much importance to the thing, but if ever those glimpses of the future, called presentiments, had foundation in truth, that young Indian is destined to exercise some sort of influence over my fate."

"You do not mean that he is to supplant Ronayne, I hope," returned her friend, trying to laugh her oat of the serious mood, in which she seemed so much inclined to indulge.

"How can you speak so, Margaret? No, my presentiment is of a different character. But it is very foolish and silly to allow the feeling to weigh with me. I will try to think more rationally. Say nothing of this, however, and least of all to Ronayne."

"Not a word, dearest. Good bye for the present. I must look after the dinner. You know who dines with us."

A look expressive of the deep sense she entertained of the consideration of her friend, was the only commentary of Miss Heywood, as she passed into her mother's apartment.

CHAPTER XI.

It was now the middle of May. A month had elapsed since the events detailed in the preceding chapters. The recollection of the outrage at Heywood's farm, committed early in April was fast dying away, save in the bosoms of those more immediately interested in the fate of its proprietor, and apprehensions of a repetition of similar atrocities had, in a great measure, ceased. A better understanding between the commanding officer and his subordinates--the result of a long private interview, which Ensign Ronayne had had with the former, on the morning after his promise to Mrs. Headley, followed by an apology on parade that day, had arisen. Corporal Nixon was now Sergeant Nixon--Collins had succeeded to him, and Le Noir and the boy--Catholic and Protestant--had been buried in one grave. Ephraim Giles filled the office of factotum to Von Vottenberg, whose love of whisky punch, was, if possible, on the increase. Winnebeg, the bearer of confidential despatches, announcing the hostile disposition and acts of certain of the Winnebagoes, had not returned, and Waunangee, who, recovered from the fumes of the claret, had, in an earnest manner, expressed to Ronayne contrition for the liberty he had taken with Miss Heywood, had departed from the neighborhood, no one knew whither. Harmony, in a word, had been some days restored in the Fort, and the only thing that detracted from the general contentment, was the uncertainty attending the fate of Mr. Heywood--regretted less, however, for his own sake, than for that of his amiable daughter, who vainly sought to conceal from her friends, the anxiety induced by an absence, the duration of which it was utterly impossible to divine. As for Mrs. Heywood, she was still in ignorance, so well had things been managed by the Elmsleys, that any of the fearful scenes had occurred. She still believed her husband to be at the farm.

But, as it was not likely she could much longer remain in ignorance of what had been the subject of conversation with every one around her, it was advised by Von Vottenberg, that, as the warmth of spring was now fully developed, and all dread of the Indians resuming their hostile visit, at an end, she should be conveyed back to the cottage, the pure air around which, was much more likely to improve her health, than the confined atmosphere of the Fort. She had accordingly been removed thither early in May, accompanied by her daughter and Catherine.

Ronayne, of course, become once more a daily visitor, and soon beneath his hand, the garden began again to assume the beautiful garb it had worn at that season, for the last two years. The interviews of the lovers here, freed from the restraints imposed upon them while in the Fort, had resumed that fervent character which had marked them on the afternoon of the day when they so solemnly interchanged their vows of undying faith. They now no longer merely looked their love. They spoke of it--drank in the sweet avowal from each others lips, and luxuriated in the sweet pleasure it imparted. They were as the whole world to each other, and although language could not convey a warmer expression of their feelings, than had already gone forth from their lips, still was the repetition replete with a sweetness that never palled upon the ear. Like the man who never tires of gazing upon his gold, so did they never tire of the treasures of the expressed love, that daily grew more intense in their hearts. And yet, notwithstanding this utter devotedness of soul--notwithstanding her flattering heart confessed in secret the fullest realization of those dreams which had filled and sustained her in early girlhood--albeit the assurance the felt that, in Ronayne, she had found the impersonation of the imaginings of her maturer life, still whenever he urged her in glowing language to name the day when she would become his wife, she evaded an answer, not from caprice, but because she would not bring to him a heart clouded by the slightest tinge of that anxiety with which ignorance of her father's fate, could not fail to shade it. A painful circumstance which happened about that period, at length, however, brought affairs to a crisis.

It was a lovely evening towards the close of May, and after a somewhat sultry morning which had been devoted to a ride on horseback along the lakeshore--Mrs. Headley and Mrs. Elmsley, who had accompanied them, having returned home, that Ronayne and his betrothed sat in the little summer-house already described. Mrs. Heywood who had been so far recovered from her weakness by the change of air, as to take slight exercise in the garden, supported by her daughter, and the young officer, had on this occasion expressed a wish to join them, in order that she might inhale the soft breeze that blew from the south, and enjoy once more the scenery of the long reach of the river, which wound its serpentine course from the direction of the farm. To this desire no other objection was offered, than what was suggested by her companions, from an apprehension that the fatigue of the ascent would be too great for her. She, however, persisted in her wish, declaring that she felt herself quite strong enough--an assertion for which her returning color gave some evidence. They ceased to oppose her. It was the first time the invalid had been in the summer-house, since the same period the preceding spring, and naturally associating the recollection of her husband, with the familiar objects in the distance, she took her daughter's hand, and said in a low and husky voice, that proved how much she had overrated her own strength:

"How is it, Maria, my love, that we have seen nothing of your father, lately? I have never known him, since we have been in this part of the country, to be so long absent from us at one time."

"Nay, dear mamma," returned the pained girl, the tears starting to her eyes, in spite of her efforts to restrain them, "I do not exactly know what can detain him. Perhaps he is not at the farm," and here her tears forced their way--"you know, dearest mamma, that he is very fond of long hunting excursions."

"Yes, but, my child, why do you weep? Surely there is nothing in that to produce such emotion. He will soon be back again."

"Oh! yes, I hope so. Forgive me, my dear mamma, but I have a very bad headache, and never felt more nervous than I do this evening. Perhaps it is the effect of my ride in the heat of the sun. Shall we go on. It is nearly sunset, and I dread your being exposed to the night-air."

"Oh! it is so delicious," softly returned the invalid; "I feel as if I had not lived for the last twelve months, until now. Only a little while longer, shall I not, Mr. Ronayne? Perhaps I may never have an opportunity of ascending to this summer-house again."

During this short conversation, trifling in itself, but conveying, under the circumstances, so much subject for deep and painful reflections, the young officer had evinced much restlessness of manner, yet without interposing any other remark than to join Miss Heywood's entreaties that her mother would suffer herself to be conducted home, before the dew should begin to fall. In order, moreover, as much as possible to leave them uninterrupted in the indulgence of their feelings, he had from the first risen, and stood with his back to them, within the entrance of the summer house, and was now, with a view to drown their conversation to his own ear, whistling to Loup Garou, sitting on his haunches outside the garden-gate, looking fixedly at him.

Touched by the account he had received of the fidelity of the dog, he, had, with the consent of Sergeant Nixon, who was glad to secure for his favorite so kind a protector, become possessed of him from the moment of his return home; and time, which had in some degree blunted the sorrow of the animal for the loss of one master, rendered equally keen his instinct of attachment for the other. Within the month he had been his, every care had been taken by Ronayne himself, as well as by his servant, to wean the mourner from the grave of Le Noir, on which, for the first few days, he had lain, absorbed in grief--refusing all food, until, yielding at length to the voice of kindness, his memory of the past seemed to have faded wholly away.

Ronayne, however, from a fear of exciting unpleasant recollections in those who were not ignorant of the former position of the dog, had endeavoured as much as possible, to prevent him from crossing the river during his visits to the cottage; but, within the last four or five days, Loup Garou would not thus be kept back, and when expelled from the boat, had swam across, taking up his station at the gate, beyond which, however, he did not presume to pass, as if sensible that the delicate parterres within, were interdicted ground, and there generally lay squatted with his nose resting on the grass, between his outstretched fore-paws, until his master came forth on his return home.

The unexpected and encouraging whistle of the latter on this occasion, which had been given in pure unconsciousness, caused him to prick his ears, and uttering a sharp cry, he sprang over the gate, bounding rapidly towards the eminence on which his master stood. About half-way between its base and the summit, there was a beautiful rose-bush which had been planted by Ronayne, and from which he had plucked two flowers, for the mother and daughter, during the ascent, and presented with a hand that was observed by Maria Heywood to tremble, and a cheek unwontedly pale.

On arriving opposite the rose-tree, the animal suddenly stopped, and putting his nose to the ground close under it, and sniffing almost furiously, uttered a prolonged and melancholy howl, while, with his fore-paws he began to scratch up the loose earth around, regardless of the voice of his master, who renewed his whistling, and called upon him almost angrily to desist.

Alarmed at this perseverance of action, the ensign descended to the spot--laid hands on Loup Garou, and sought to remove him, but the animal, strong of neck--full in the chest--and on the present occasion, under the influence of furious impulse, was not to be restrained.

The moaning of the dog--the descent-the corrective voice of his master, and the seeming struggle of both to attain opposite purposes, naturally attracted the attention of those above, and they both rose and neared to the doorway Ronayne had so recently quitted. Their horror may well be imagined when, on looking down, they found that the dog had already uncovered a human body, which, though disfigured and partially decomposed, filial and conjugal affection too clearly distinguished as the father of the one, the husband of the other!

Uttering a feeble shriek, Mrs. Heywood fell insensible within the threshold of the summer-house, while her daughter, less overwhelmed, but with feelings impossible to describe, stooped and chafed her mother's temples, and notwithstanding a horrid thought, which, despite her own will, shot through her mind, that the man to whom she had given every affection of her heart, was in some degree connected with this horrid spectacle, she called vehemently to him for assistance.

The situation of the perplexed officer was scarcely less painful. On the one hand, feeling all the necessity of retaining his grasp of Loup Garou, as the only means of preventing him from further uncovering of the body--on the other, urged by the summons of her, whom he knew, from her very manner, to be in possession of this fearful secret, his mind become a perfect chaos, and large drops of perspiration streamed from his brow. In this irritating dilemma, a sudden transport of rage took possession of his heart, and seizing Loup Garou with both his hands, he so compressed them around his throat, that the dog, already exhausted with his exertions, was half-strangled before being raised with a frantic effort, and dashed with violence upon the body he had so unhappily been instrumental in discovering.

Scarcely had this been done--a low moaning from Loup Garou, as if reproaching him for the act, alone denoting that he breathed, when the ensign flew up the steps of the summer-house, and regardless of the involuntary half-shudder of his betrothed, as he approached, caught the insensible invalid in his arms, and so carrying her, that her eyes, if she should open them, could not encounter the horrid spectacle below, again rapidly descended, and hurried towards the house. Maria Heywood, on passing the rose-tree so recently prized, but now so abhorrent to her sight, could not resist a strong impulse to look upon the mysteries so strangely unveiled, but although the twilight had not yet passed away, nothing could be seen but the displaced earth, and stretched over the excavation he himself had made, the motionless body of the dog.

Sick at heart, and with wild and unconnected images floating through her heated brain, she followed almost mechanically to the cottage.

This was no time for ceremony. When answering the loud ring, Catherine appeared hurriedly at the door, Ronayne bore his inanimate charge into her bedroom, and in silence and deep grief, sought, by every means in his power, to restore her. But all his efforts proving vain, he, in a state of mind difficult to describe, tore a leaf from his pocket-book, wrote a few hurried lines to Elmsley, requesting him to allow his wife to come over immediately with Von Vottenberg, and when they had departed, to call upon Captain Headley and explain the cause of his absence. This note he gave to Catherine, with instructions to cross in the boat which was waiting for himself, and to return with Mrs. Elmsley, or if she did not come, with the doctor.

When left together, beside the insensible body of Mrs. Heywood, the lovers experienced for the first time, a feeling of restraint, for in the hearts of both, were passing thoughts which neither seemed desirous of imparting. But, Maria Heywood, gentle as she was, was not of a character long to endure the state of uncertainty under which she labored. The strange wild apprehensions which had arisen, she knew not how or why, had so preyed upon her quiet, that suspense became intolerable, and at length, addressing her lover in a voice, never more melancholy or touching than at that moment, and looking at him with an expression of deep sadness, while the large tears trickled down her cheeks.

"Ronayne, you know--you must have known--your whole conduct throughout this affair, proves you must have known of my poor father's death, and of his rude--almost insulting burial in that fatal spot. How he came hither, you best can tell. Oh!

Harry, it is very cruel thus to have reposed the confidence of the entire soul, and then to have been disappointed. This cruel discovery will be the means of destroying my peace forever, unless you give the explanation which alone can restore our confidence in each other--yet how can I, with these glaring truths before my eyes, expect that you will?"

"Insulting burial! oh, Maria, I feel that I never loved you more than now when you would break my heart with this unkindness." He bent his head upon the same pillow, upon which reclined the unconscious head of the mother of the woman whom he so ardently loved, and wept tears of bitterness and sorrow.

"I cannot stand this, Ronayne, dear Ronayne, whatever you be--whatever you may have done, I love you with all the ardor of the most devoted soul! But," she continued, more composedly, "forgive me, if my feelings and my judgment are at issue. One question I must ask, cost what it may, for I cannot longer endure this agony of suspense --no, for your sake I cannot endure it. How is it that you have always made a secret--a mystery even to me, of the motive of your absence on that fatal night succeeding the massacre at the firm."

"Dear Maria. I can well forgive the question in the excitement which must have been produced in you by the startling events of this evening."

"Ronayne," she mournfully interrupted--"your sudden interference with the dog--your struggle with him--nay, your very manner of speaking now, convince me that you knew my father lay buried beneath that rose-tree. In candor, answer me. Yes or no."

"And, admitting I had had that knowledge, Maria--can you imagine no good reason for my forbearing all allusion to the subject?"

"Yet, why conceal the fact from one who had supposed you could have no concealment from her--and then again, how am I to reconcile the circumstance of my poor father having been reported to be a prisoner--a report which, sanctioned by yourself, left me not utterly hopeless--and the fact of his burial here--evidently with your knowledge."

"Maria," returned Ronayne, impressively, and with an expression of much pain at the remark, "as I have already said, I can make every allowance, in recollection of the painful scene of which I have, in some degree, been the cause, but is it generous--is it quite appreciating my character and my feelings towards yourself, to doubt that I had intended from the first, and at a fitting moment, to explain every thing to you?"

Again was the confidence of the generous girl established, and with almost passionate warmth, she exclaimed. "Oh! Ronayne, forgive--forgive me, but this melancholy--this harrowing occurrence has made me so far not myself--that I almost hate myself. Tell me, dear Ronayne, do you forgive me?"

"Yes, from the bottom of my soul, do I forgive you, and yet, dearest, there is nothing to forgive, for how could it be otherwise, than that your poor and sorely tried heart should be subjected to wild imaginings inexplicable to yourself. The ordeal to which you have been submitted, is a severe one, but I am sure your oppressed heart will be greatly lightened when you shall have been in possession of the truth connected with this most melancholy affair-- your regard for me, will if possible, be even greater than before. Pardon this seeming vanity. I make the assertion because I know it will not a little console you, under this terrible infliction."

It was a strange sight, that of these lovers, hitherto so devoted and now only temporarily half-doubting, talking of the fate of one parent while leaning over the apparent death-bed of the other.

"Ronayne, dear Ronayne, I am satisfied--fully, wholly satisfied, and as you observe, the assurance which you have now given me, will form my chief support under this double affliction," and she pointed, weeping, to her mother, whose scarcely perceptible breathing alone attested that she lived.

"Maria," he said tenderly and gravely, as he took her hand in his, over the invalid--"the hour of your promise is come--the fate of your father is known--would that it had been less abruptly revealed--and were other inducement to keep it wanting, is it not to be found here? But at this moment I will ask nothing which you may feel reluctance in granting. To-morrow we will speak of this again--to-morrow you shall know how much I have sought--how much I have risked--to soften the pang which I knew would, soon or late be inflicted on her whom I so love."

"Generous--kind--considerate Ronayne, I can fully understand you, yet, ah! what must you think of me, who could for a moment doubt your power to explain every act of your life, however ambiguous in appearance. But what is that paper you have taken from your pocket-book?"

"One that I have long designed for your perusal. It was written a few days after the events at the farm, and I have since then frequently determined to place it in your hands in order that, in the sacredness of solitude, you might indulge in the bitter tears its few pages will wring from you; but too selfish--yes, selfish, and severely am I punished for it--to suffer the joy of the hour to be broken in upon by sadness, I have hitherto delayed putting you in possession of that which, if only communicated a day earlier, would have spared us this painful scene. But I hear footsteps approaching. They must be those of Mrs. Elmsley and the doctor, with Catherine. Be not surprised, dearest, if I leave you soon after they enter, for I have something to do this evening which will require my presence in the Fort. Early in the morning, however, I shall be here."

"I understand well what demands your presence elsewhere," she returned with a look of deep gratitude and love. "Oh! Ronayne, whatever may happen," and the tears streamed down her pale face, as she pointed to her mother--"hear me declare that whatever you may ask of me one month hence, I shall not consider myself justified in refusing."

Scarcely had he time to impress upon her lips his deep but chastened sense of happiness, when the party expected, entered the room--Von Vottenberg immediately applying himself to an examination of the patient, whose condition, it was evident from his unusually grave look, he conceived to be highly critical.

Dreading to hear his opinion pronounced in the presence of his betrothed, and the more so, because he had in some degree been its cause, the young officer, after having warmly shaken hands with Mrs. Elmsley, whom he thanked for her prompt attention, urged her to do all in her power to soothe Maria, to whom, at parting, he also offered his hand, while his eye was eloquent with the feelings he could not well openly express.

He first directed his course towards the rose-bush, and approached it with a feeling almost similar to what would have been experienced by him, had he been the actual murderer of Mr. Heywood. Loup Garou was sitting crouched near the head and was so far recovered as to growl rather fiercely at him, as he approached. On hearing the voice of his master, not in anger but in conciliation, he arose, slightly wagged his tail, and came forward slowly and crouching, as if in dread of further punishment, his lip uncurled, showing all his upper teeth, and with a short, quick sneeze, peculiar to his half-wolf-blooded race.

Calling gently to the animal, he preceded him to the gate, desiring him to wait there until he returned--an injunction evidently understood by the dog, which, crouching down in his accustomed posture, ventured not to move. With the small spud, already alluded to, and then near the rose-tree, he put back in small quantities the displaced earth, until the ghastly face, indistinctly seen in the star-light, was again wholly hidden from view. This done, he approached the bank of the river, followed by the dog, and gave a shrill whistle, which, without being answered, speedily brought over the boat in which he now embarked for the opposite shore.

His first care was to seek Elmsley, who, as officer of the guard, was up accoutred for duty, and was now looking over an old "Washington Intelligencer," that had been read at least a dozen times before, while he smoked his pipe and sipped from a bowl of whisky punch, which Von Vottenberg had just finished brewing, when so suddenly summoned to the cottage.

After Ronayne had detailed to his friend the occurrences of the evening, and communicated his views, they both issued forth to the guard-room, where Sergeant Nixon happened to be upon duty. With the latter, a brief conversation was held by Ronayne, ending with an injunction for him to come to Lieutenant Elmsley's quarters and announce to him (the former), when certain arrangements which had been agreed upon, were completed.

Returned to the abode of the latter, the young officer required no very great pressing to induce him to join his superior in the beverage, to which anxiety of mind not less than fatigue of body had so much disposed him, yet of which both partook moderately. While so employed, and awaiting the appearance of the sergeant, Ronayne, who had now no motive for further mystery or concealment, detailed at the request of his friend, but in much more succinct terms than he had done in the paper he had handed to Maria Heywood, the circumstances connected with his absence from the Fort, on the night of the attack upon the farm, and the means taken by him to attain the object in which he had been thwarted by Captain Headley.

CHAPTER XII.

"Y ou dam Yankee, stop Injin when him go wigwam," commenced Ronayne, rising at the same time and imitating the action of one unsteady from intoxication. "'Spose tell him gubbernor?"

"Ah! you horrid wretch--I see it all now, yet could I have been so imposed upon? You then were the pretended drunken Indian I let out that night? Upon my word, Master Ronayne. I never will forgive you for that trick."

"Yes you will, old fellow. It was the only way to save you from a scrape, but I confess I have often since laughed in my sleeve at the recollection of the manner in which I deceived you."

"Hang me if you didn't play your part to admiration, but the best of the jest is, that on reporting the circumstance to Headley, on the following morning, he said I had acted perfectly right; so had you known this when you had that scene on the parade, you might have pleaded his sanction. However, all that is over. Now then for your adventure."

"The tale is soon told," began Ronayne. "On the evening when you and Von Vottenberg were so busy, the one in concocting his whisky-punch--the other in cutting up the Virginia, I was sacking my brain for a means to accomplish my desire to reach the farm, where I had a strong presentiment, from the lateness of the hour, without bringing any tidings of them, the fishing-party were, with Mr. Heywood and his people, in a state of siege, and I at length decided on what seemed to me to be the only available plan. I was not sorry to see you leave after taking your second glass, for I knew that I should have little difficulty in sewing up the doctor, whose tumbler I repeatedly filled, and made him drink off after sundry toasts, while he did not perceive--or was by no means sorry if he did--that I merely sipped from my own. When I thought he had swallowed enough to prevent him from interfering with my project, I bade him good night and left him, knowing well that in less than ten minutes he would be asleep. Instead, however, of going to bed, I hastened at once to preliminaries, having first got rid of my servant whom I did not wish to implicate, by making him acquainted with my intended absence. But tell me, did you examine my room at all the next day?"

"I did."

"And found nothing missing?"

"Nothing. I scouted everywhere, and found only yourself wanting--the bed unrumpled, and everything in perfect bachelor order."

"And that leather dress, my dear fellow, in which I once paid a visit to the camp of Winnebeg, from whose squaw, indeed, I had bought it. You know it generally hangs against the wall at the foot of my bed."

"Ah! now I recollect, that was not there certainly, although I did not notice its absence then--so then, that was the dress you went out in, and I such a goose as not to remark it."

"Because you know that I had had the precaution to throw a blanket over it in the most approved Pottawattamie style, while my features were colored with gambouge and Indian ink."

"Well, say no more about that--I am ashamed to have been so taken in by a Johnny Raw. We will now suppose you kicked out of the Fort. Did I not kick you out," he added humorously, "and say, begone, you drunken dog, and never show your ugly face here again!"

"On the contrary," returned his junior in the same mocking strain, "you were but too glad to be civil when I threatened you with the 'gubbernor!'"

"Once out of the Fort," he gravely continued, "my course was plain. I immediately went to the wigwam of Winnebeg, whom I found seated, with his toes almost in the embers of an expiring fire, and smoking his last pipe previous to wrapping himself up for the night in his blanket. You may imagine his surprise, when, after some little difficulty, he recognized in that garb, and at that hour, particularly after the events of the day, with which he had been made acquainted by Mr. Frazer, before the latter, with his family, took refuge in the Fort. Still, true to the dignified reserve of his race, he concealed as much as possible what was passing in his mind, and made me sit by his side, near which, I have omitted to say, was an extremely handsome young Indian, whom he presented to me as his son, and then bade me tell him the object of my visit.

"Of course I knew enough of Indian etiquette to be satisfied that I should gain by not attempting to hurry matters, and I accordingly suppressed my own impatience while taking a few whiffs from the pipe he courteously offered to me. Winnebeg then received it back, and while he sat with his eyes fixed intently on the fire, puffed away in an attitude of profound attention which encouraged me to proceed.

"When he had heard all I had to say in regard to the fears I entertained for the absent party--for I did not confine my profession of interest to ONE--my vain application to the commandant, and my strong reliance upon him to send a party of his young men with me to the farm, his eye suddenly kindled--his countenance assumed a more animated expression, and removing the pipe from his lips, and puffing forth a more than usual volume of smoke, he cordially shook my hands, saying something in Indian to his son, who immediately sprang to his feet, and disappeared from the tent.

"After a lapse of time which seemed to me as an age, the youth re-appeared with a dozen young warriors, all armed and decked in their war paint. They remained grouped round the entrance for a few minutes, while Waunangee changed his own dress, and Winnebeg provided me with a rifle, tomahawk and scalping-knife. Thus accoutred I took the lead with the former, and after cautiously creeping through the encampment, passed along the skirt of the wood that almost overhung the river. We moved off at a quick walk, but soon our pace increased to a half-run, so anxious were we all to get to the farm.

"We had not proceeded more than half-way when we saw a small boat, which I immediately distinguished as that belonging to the fishing-party, slowly descending the river. The Indians simultaneously, and as if governed by one common instinct, dropped flat on the ground, as I supposed to remain unseen until the boat should come opposite to them, while I, uncertain by whom it was occupied, and anxious to ascertain, after whispering a few words to Waunangee, moved cautiously in advance along the shore. When I had crept up about fifty yards, I could distinctly see that it was one of our men, and I immediately hailed to know who he was, and where the remainder of the party were.

"Scarcely had he answered 'Collins,' and commenced a few words of explanation of the cause of his being there and alone, when the forms of two Indians, which I fancied I had before detected creeping along the shore, regulating their stealthy progress by that of the boat, started into full height, and silently bounded towards me--one a little in advance of the other. The moment was critical. They were not twenty paces from me, and I have often since wondered at the presence of mind I preserved. It occurred to me that they would not commit the imprudence of using firearms so near the Fort, and that steel only would be resorted to by them. This suggested my own course. Throwing my rifle upon the beach in order that Collins, who was now pulling for the shore, might seize and use it as occasion should require, I grasped the scalping-knife in my left hand, and with my tomahawk in my right, did not wait for the attack, but rushed upon the foremost Indian, for I knew that my only chance of success lay in the killing or disabling of one before his comrade could come up. At the same time, both to apprise Waunangee of my position, and to daunt my adversaries, I uttered one of these tremendous yells, you know I so well can imitate, and receiving the blow of his tomahawk upon my own, thrown up in true military guard, plunged my knife into his body with such suddenness and force, that on examining it afterwards, I found that at least half an inch of the tapering handle had followed the blade. The savage fell dead without uttering a groan, a sight which, instead of checking the advance of his companion, rather urged him to revenge his fall. He had now come up with me, brandishing his tomahawk, when I put myself again on my guard, purposing to use my knife as I had done before, but at the very moment when the descent of his weapon was expected by me, he was suddenly seized from behind, raised from his feet, and thrown upon the ground. This was the act of Collins, who had gained the shore just after the first Indian fell, and had flown to my assistance.

"At the same moment, Waunangee, who, with his warriors had started up on hearing my loud yell of defiance, came quickly to the spot, and they were not a little astounded to see an Indian, whom they instantly pronounced to be a Winnebago, lying motionless at my feet, nor was their respect for me at all lessened, when on handing my scalping-knife from one to the other, they perceived what a proficient I was in the use of their own favorite weapon.

"Of course I was not silly enough to detract from my own glory, by admitting that it was as much the result of accident as of design. They made signs for me to scalp him, but having no particular desire to possess this trophy of my successful hand to hand encounter, one of the young men asked me to waive my right in his favor. This I did, and the scalp of the Winnebago was soon dangling from his waist. The other spoils I did not object to, and his rifle, tomahawk, and knife are now in Winnebago's tent, until there offers a favorable opportunity of bringing them to my quarters. But to proceed.

"So much time had been passed in the examination of the body of the slain Winnebago, that his comrade had found ample time to escape. The Pottawattamies had not seen him, and Collins, after having temporarily disabled him, had run up to afford me further assistance, on seeing advancing in the rear, those whom he took to be of the same hostile party. Thus left unwatched, the savage had managed to creep away into the wood, and when attention was at length drawn to him, he was not to be seen.

"When Collins had explained the position of the party at the farm, whose danger, on finding himself of no service there, he was then on his way to report, I proposed to Waunangee that half of his warriors should ascend by land, while the remainder with himself, accompanied me in the boat. We accordingly separated, and made what haste we could to our destination--the party on shore regulating their progress by that of the boat. During the descent my anxiety was very great, for my whole soul was bent upon the attainment of one object--that of restoring Mr. Heywood unharmed to his family. But the absence of all sound indicating conflict was by no means favorable, and I had already begun to fear that the silence which prevailed, was but the result of victory on the part of the hostile band who had departed, when suddenly the loud, fierce yell of disappointment which burst from them, as I have since understood, when a ladder by which they attempted to enter was thrown from the roof by Nixon, rang encouragingly upon my ear, and urged me to increased exertion. Our progress, however, was by no means proportioned to my anxiety, for somehow or other, only two oars were in the boat, and, as the Indians did not much care or know how to pull in time, the task devolved wholly upon Collins and myself. At length, just as the day was beginning to dawn, we reached the farm-house, about a hundred yards beyond which we put in and landed, making a detour by the barn, so as to meet the remainder of our little force in the rear, and thus to place the enemy, if actually surrounding the house, between two fires.

"After waiting, however, some little time, and finding every thing quiet, my apprehensions increased, for, although not the sign of a Winnebago could be seen, so profound was the stillness within, that I began to think the whole of the party had been either captured or murdered. Suddenly, however, while hesitating as to the course to be pursued--for I feared that if the party were all right, and the enemy departed, they might fire upon us as we approached--I saw a man in American undress uniform, whom I had no difficulty in recognizing as Corporal Nixon, issue from the back of the house with a basket in his hands, and turning the corner with an appearance of much caution, make hastily for the river. Directing Waunangee, whose two bands had now joined, and were then lying closely concealed in the barn, to enter the house as cautiously and noiselessly as possible, I hastened after Nixon, from whom, after recovering from his first fright at finding himself unarmed, and in the power of one whom he naturally took for one of his recent assailants, I received a brief account of all that had occurred. On entering the house with him, shortly afterwards, what a contrast was present--on the one hand the ludicrous--the horrible on the other.

"Close within the doorway lay the dead body of Mr. Heywood--"

"The dead body of Mr. Heywood!" exclaimed Elmsley, starting from his chair in almost dismay at the intelligence. "How comes it, Ronayne, that you have never spoken of this before?"

"No interruption, Elmsley--hear me to the close--close within the doorway, I repeat, lay the dead body of Mr. Heywood--his face much disfigured--and his large frame almost rigid in a pool of clotted blood. Imagine what a sight this was to me, whose sole object and hope it had been to restore the father in safety to the daughter, although at intervals during the route, I had more than once dreaded something of the sort. Stupefied at the spectacle, I felt my heart to sicken, as the idea of the grief by which Maria would be overwhelmed when this sad tale should be revealed to her, rose to my imagination. But even then my presence of mind did not desert me, and I already determined on what was to be done. In some degree consoled by this, I raised my glance from the body to observe what further atrocity had been committed. Three or four Indians were grouped around, evidently regarding the corpse with deep interest, for Mr. Heywood had often hunted with them, and given them refreshments when stopping to rest at his place, while on their way to the Fort laden with game. Further on the great body of Waunangee's people were standing leaning on their rifles, and enjoying the mistake of three of our fellows, who naturally taking them, from the great resemblance of dress, to be their enemies who had obtained an entrance, were holding aloft, in an attitude of defiance--one a huge poker thrust through the carcass of an enormous bird, and two others a blackened leg and wing, evidently belonging to the same animal, which they ever and anon brandished over their heads, while their eyes were rivetted on the dusky forms before them. The wooden partition sustained their muskets, from which the interposing Indians had cut them off, and against the front door of the house, which was closed and barred, leaned the only armed man of the party, deprived, however, of all power of action."

"What a scene for some American Hogarth!" interrupted the lieutenant, "and how graphically you have described it. I can see the picture before me now."

"I confess," answered Ronayne, "I could not even, amid all my own painful feelings, suppress a smile at its extreme absurdity, for the appearance of three men seeking to defend themselves from what they believed to be fierce and blood-thirsty enemies, with the burnt carcass and limbs of an old turkey-cock, was such a burlesque on the chivalrous, that, knowing as I did how little their supposed enemy was to be dreaded, I could not suppress thoughts which, while they forced themselves upon me, I was angry at allowing myself to entertain. To understand the scene fully, you must have looked on it yourself. Had I recounted this to you yesterday, or even this morning, I could have filled up the picture more grotesquely, and yet not less truly. But now I have too great a weight on my spirits to give more than a simple sketch.

"At the announcement of my name and purpose, the statue at the door became suddenly disenchanted--the legs and wings fell--a man dropped lightly from the loft, musket in hand, and Cass only, with his gaze intently fixed on the mocking savages before him, of whom he took me indeed to be one, continued his defensive attitude with the poker, nor was it until I had advanced and taken his weapon from him, amid the loud laughter of the young Indians, that he finally came to his senses. And yet, after all, poor devil, his distrust was but natural.

"No time was to be lost. While some of the men were, according to my instructions, wrapping in a blanket the body of Mr. Heywood, after removing from it what blood they could, and the others bore to the boat the unfortunate Le Noir, whom

I had not at first distinguished, so completely had he been covered over by his dog and walnut blossoms, I took the corporal aside, and explained to him how important it was that nothing should be known at the Fort of the fate of Mr. Heywood. On his asking what he should say if questioned, I desired him (with some hesitation, I confess, for I knew I was setting a bad example to the men, which only the peculiar circumstances of the case could justify), to give an evasive answer, and say that the Indians had carried him off with them, which indeed would be the fact, as I intended him to be borne away by the party I had brought. I told him, moreover, that at a fitting opportunity, I would explain every thing to Captain Headley, and take all the responsibility upon myself.

"On his promptly saying that he would, I added that the men of his party should be made acquainted with my wish, and asked if I might depend upon their secrecy. He replied that there was not a man among them who did not so love Miss Heywood, as to run the risk of any punishment, rather than utter one word that could be the means of giving her pain, and that while on the way down he would take care to warn them.

"Elmsley, I was touched at this--almost to tears--for it was a source of proud yet tender pleasure to me--much more so than I can express--to know that Maria was so great a favorite with these rude-hearted fellows. Assured that every thing was right, I told the corporal to embark his men immediately, and pull for the Fort, while I, with Waunangee and his Indians proceeded by land with the body of Mr. Heywood.

"'Don't you think, sir,' said the corporal, hesitatingly, as he prepared to execute my orders--'don't you think it would be well for the ladies' sake that they should not be reminded of the name of this place, more than can be helped?'

"'Undoubtedly, Nixon, but what do you mean?'

"'Why, sir, I mean that as poor Mr. Heywood never can be here again, it would be better nothing should be left to remind them of the bloody doings of yesterday.'

"'And what other name would you give it?' I asked.

"'If it was left to me, Mr. Ronayne,' replied the corporal; 'I would call it HARD-SCRABBLE, on account of the hard struggle the fellows must have had with Mr. Heywood, judging from his wounds and his broken rifle, before they mastered him.'

"'Then, HARDSCRABBLE be it,' I said, 'not that I can really see it will make much difference in calling the thing to mind, yet it would scarcely be fair to deny to you, who have so bravely defended the place, the privilege of giving it a new name, if the old one is to be abandoned.'

"'Thank you, sir,' returned Nixon, 'but if you hadn't come to our assistance, I don't know what the upshot might have been, I suspect that fellow whose comrade you killed, sent them off sooner than they intended.'

"'No more of that, Nixon--and now do you remember what you are to say when you get back to the Fort?'

"'I do, sir, and every man shall be told to say as I do--but about the new name, Mr. Ronayne,' he pursued, returning, after he had gone a few paces, 'do you think, sir, Mrs. Heywood will consent to it?'

"'My good fellow,' I answered, 'recollect that Mrs. Heywood must know nothing about it--at least for the present. I will settle all that later. In the mean time, as you have called it HARDSCRABBLE, so let it remain.'

"And HARDSCRABBLE that scene of blood is called to this hour.

"I had at first apprehended," pursued Ronayne, "that the Indians would evince disinclination to carry the body so long a distance, or even at all, but on Waunangee explaining my desire, they all to my surprise, expressed even eagerness to meet my wishes, for, as he assured me, the young men looked upon me as a great warrior who had achieved a deed of heroism that might procure the distinction of a chief, and entitling me to their services in all things.

"I certainly thought my honors cheaply enough purchased; however I was but too glad to appropriate to myself the respect and good-will which the killing of the Winnebago had entailed--and matters were soon arranged.

"The body having been removed outside, and the doors secured as well as, under the circumstances, could be done, one of the warriors cut from a tree in the adjacent wood, a semi-circular piece of tough and flexible bark, about six feet in length, and in the hollow of this, the murdered father of Maria Heywood, already swathed tightly in a blanket, was placed. A long pole was then passed through the equi-distant loops of cord that encircled the whole, and two of the Indians having, with the assistance of their companions, raised it upon their shoulders, it was thus borne--the parties being relieved at intervals--over the two long miles of road that led to the skirt of the woods near the encampment. Here the body of Indians stopped, while Waunangee and myself repaired to the tent of his father, who no sooner had heard detailed by his son the account of my Winnebago killing practice of the preceding evening, than he overwhelmed me with congratulations, and looked proudly on the knife, still stained with a spot or two of blood, which I returned to him, and which he restored to its usual resting-place on his hip.

"Perceiving that Winnebeg was, like his young men, ready to do any thing for me. I explained to him my desire to convey the body of Mr. Heywood across the river, and bury him secretly in his own grounds, but that it was necessary, in order to do this effectually, that he and his son should go with me, and by some circuitous route. Entering at once into my views, he said he would show me a place where we could cross without being seen either from the Fort or from his own encampment, and then led the way back to the wood where the party were still waiting.

"The rest is soon told. Dismissing the young men into the encampment. Winnebeg, with his son, bore the body within the skirt of the wood, until we reached a bend of the river hidden from observation, where a canoe with paddles was drawn up on the beach. There we crossed, and going round to the rear of the cottage, entered the garden, and proceeded to the upper end, where at the summer house, near a favorite rose-tree of Maria's, I dug with my own hands a hasty grave, in which Winnebeg and Waunangee placed the body--its only coffin being the bark that was swathed around it. Of course I always intended to disinter it at some future, but not distant period, and bestow upon it the usual rites of burial.

"This painful task accomplished, and the soil having been carefully replaced, so as to leave no inequality of surface, I accompanied my friends back by the same route, and about nine o'clock left the Pottawattamie encampment with them and a few other warriors of the tribe for the Fort, which in the crowd I entered without difficulty or creating suspicion. Watching my opportunity, I stole to the rear of my bed-room--opened and entered the window-- changed my dress, and made my appearance on parade as you saw."

"All is ready, sir," said Sergeant Nixon, entering just as he had concluded, and before Elmsley could offer any remark on this singular adventure--"the coffin is in the scow, and Corporal Collins, Green and Philips are there also with their shovels, ropes, and picks. If Mr. Elmsley will give me permission," and he touched his cap to that officer. "I will go too, sir."

"As sergeant of the guard--no, Nixon, my good fellow, that will never do. The three men you have named, are, with myself, quite enough. Be on the look-out though, to let us in on our return. Have you provided a dark lantern?"

"Yes, sir, Collins has the lantern belonging to the guard house."

"Good. I will follow you in a moment, Elmsley," he continued, rising and draining off his half-emptied glass, "lend me your prayer-book. I wish that you could be present at this dismal ceremony, but of course that is wholly out of the question."

"It is, indeed, my dear fellow. It would never do for us both to be absent. Not only ourselves but the men would be brought into the scrape, for you know Headley always sleeps with one eye open."

"I do not like to do any thing clandestinely," remarked the ensign--"particularly after our reconciliation with him. Moreover, it is, as you say, in some degree compromising the men and myself with them. I have a great mind before I start to see and explain every thing to Headley, and obtain his sanction to my absence."

"Nonsense," returned his friend, "he will never know it; besides it is possible that he may refuse to let you go before morning, and your object is, of course, to have every thing finished to-night. Take my advice; go without speaking to him on the subject, and if your remorse of conscience," and he smiled archly, "be so great afterwards, as to deprive you of more rest and appetite than you lost after killing that poor devil of a Winnebago, go to him as you did before--confess that you have again been a naughty boy--ask his pardon, and I am sure he will forgive the crime."

"Well, I believe you are right. Be it so. Adieu, I shall be back within a couple of hours at the latest."

"If you do, you will in all probability find me still poring over this old Intelligencer, which is full of rumors of approaching war with the British."

"I shall be more inclined to hug my pillow," replied the ensign as he departed, "for I must again cross to the cottage, and be back here before guard-mounting to-morrow."

Within ten minutes the party--two of them having borne the empty coffin, and the corporal the necessary implements, stood near the rose-tree in the garden. The body of Mr. Heywood was disinterred--the bark in which it lay wound round with many folds of a large sheet, and placed in the coffin, which after being screwed down, was deposited in a grave dug at least five feet under the surface. Then commenced the burial service, which was read by the young officer in a slow and impressive tone, and by the light of the shaded lantern, which, falling obliquely upon the forms of the men, discovered them standing around the grave--one foot resting on the edge--the other drawn back, as they awaited the signal to lower their almost offensive burden into its last resting-place. At length the prayers for the dead were ended, and the grave was carefully filled up, leaving as before, no inequality, but too deep to attract the scent of Loup Garou. Then after having dug up a few small roots of the sweet briar, and placed them at intervals on the newly-turned earth. Ronayne crossed with his little party to the Fort, glad to obtain a few hours of that repose, for which the harassing events of the day had so much predisposed him.

CHAPTER XIII.

The fourth of July 1812, was a more than usual gala-day in the little Fort of Chicago, for in addition to the National Jubilee, there was to be celebrated one of a private, yet not less interesting nature. On that evening Ensign Ronayne was to espouse, in the very room in which he had first been introduced to her the woman he had so long and so ardently loved, and who, her mother having after a severe struggle become convalescent, had conformably to her promise, yielded a not reluctant consent to his proposal that this day of general joy, should be that of the commencement of their own happiness.

At that remote period, and in the absence of duly ordained clergymen, it was customary for marriages to be performed by the Governors of Districts and by commanding officers of distant Forts, and these, perfectly legal, were subsequently as inclination, or scruple of conscience induced, celebrated in the usual manner. The early marriages of British subjects in Canada, soon after its conquest from the French, as well as many of those of the colonies now known as the United States, took place in this manner, and the custom had been continued until increased population provided the means of securing that spiritual comfort, which it must, of course, have been impossible for one dressed in a red coat instead of a black one, to impart.

But neither Maria Heywood or Ronayne stood much on this punctilio. Provided the ceremony was legal, and according to the customs of the country, it mattered little who married them--the governor of a district--the commandant of a garrison, or a Gretna Green blacksmith--had they felt at all disposed to avail themselves of the services of the latter.

It was a lovely day, and every thing seemed to smile upon the denizens of that region, from the early dawn until the setting of the sun. Officers and men were in their brightest uniforms--the women and children in their holiday dresses. A splendid new Star Spangled Banner--the work of Maria Heywood's hands--floated in the dazzling rays of the sun, upon the southern bastion of the Fort. Joy and pride sat on every brow. They exulted at the recollection of that hardly won freedom from injustice, which was that day to be celebrated for the thirty-sixth time.

At noon the cannon thundered forth their bursts of rejoicing. This was the signal for the numerous Pottawattamies outside, all of whom had decked themselves for the occasion, to approach nearer to the Fort. On the glacis they discharged their guns and rifles, and seemed to have but one spirit with the allies to whom they appeared to have devoted themselves. Winnebeg, however, though long expected, had not yet returned, and nothing yet had been seen of Waunangee, since his departure on the day following the little incident which occurred in Elmsley's apartments.

Contrary to that unnatural etiquette which enjoins that two betrothed persons, who are expected to be inseparable after marriage, should never show themselves together in public immediately before, Ronayne had after parade ascended the rampart, with Maria Heywood leaning upon his arm, occasionally glancing at the group of gaily-costumed Indians, who were amusing themselves on the green, but oftener admiring the lovely view, softened by distance, which was presented in various points, and particularly towards the farm--the theatre of events which the otherwise happy girl, could not at that moment avoid bringing to her recollection.

While gazing in that direction, her eye fell upon the form of a young Indian who was leaning against the corner of the picketed bastion on her left, in the shallow, dry, and grass-covered ditch that surrounded it. At first her glance caught an indistinct human form dressed in the Indian garb, but as her gaze settled on the object, her surprise was great to recognise Waunangee, who was even then looking at her with the same softened and eloquent expression, which had given her so much anxiety on a former occasion. The impression produced upon her was exactly what it had been then--indescribable--inexplicable to herself.

"What is the matter, my love?" inquired Ronayne tenderly, and pressing her arm to his heart--"what fixes your attention below?" then seeing the Indian himself. "Ah! Waunangee, my friend!" he exclaimed, "where have you been all this time? Come round to the gate and shake hands with my wife."

"No, no, no, do not call him up, Ronayne--you cannot think how much the presence of that Indian troubles me."

"Nay, dearest Maria, you are not yourself. Why continue this strong dislike against the poor fellow? I thought you had quite forgiven him."

Was it accident--was it modesty, or was it a consciousness that his presence was not desired by at least one of the parties, that prevented the young Indian from obeying the summons of the officer. Whatever the cause, he assumed a serious mein, and playing one of those melancholy airs which so often, at that time, might be heard proceeding from the rude flute of their race, walked slowly away.

"I fear you have offended him, Maria. Oh! if you knew--"

"Ronayne--dearest Harry!" interrupted his betrothed--"I have never said anything of this before to you, because, after all, it is but an idle fancy, yet I cannot divest myself of the idea that this Indian, interesting and prepossessing as he is, is somehow or other connected with my future fate. Nay," as the young officer smiled in playful mockery, "you may ridicule my presentiment, which is, I confess, so much at variance with good sense, that I almost blush to introduce the subject, but still I cannot banish the impression."

"Then, I will assist you in doing so, dearest, even though at the risk of re-opening a newly-closed wound," remarked her lover, with deep affection of manner. "In my narrative of those events, hastily thrown together, which I gave you on that memorable night, when I suffered for a period, almost the torments of the damned, I did not, it seems to me, name the young Indian, who, with his father, so greatly aided me on my return to the farm, and even bore upon his shoulders the sacred charge."

"No, Harry, you did not," quickly rejoined Maria Heywood; "but I know now whom you mean. It was Waunangee."

"It was," said the ensign--"I know your knowledge of that fact will change your feelings towards him."

"They are changed--even at this moment, and henceforth I shall be to him as a sister. Ah! how ungrateful must I have appeared to the poor fellow. I shall conquer this silly weakness: I have misunderstood my own impressions, and it must have been that I have mistaken the influence Waunangee has had for that which is to be. Call him up now, Ronayne, and I will cheerfully give him my hand, and promise to love him as a brother in return for the devotion he has evinced, not less for you than for my poor father."

"Time enough, repentant sinner," returned the young officer, at the same time casting his glance rapidly over the group of Indians, who were amusing themselves at various athletic games. "I can see nothing of him. Your evident displeasure," he added playfully, "has destroyed his peace, as indeed you might have known from that plaintive ditty. However, dearest girl, I shall see him soon, and make him promise to be present this evening at the nuptials of his friend and sister. Nay, if I had not engaged Elmsley, I should insist on his being my bridesman."

The only notice taken of this sally was a faint smile from his companion, who now descended with him from the rampart and proceeded to the apartments of Mrs. Elmsley, where her mother and herself had once more been visitors for the last few days. Here they separated to meet again in the evening--Ronayne directing his attention to his various duties, and looking out at intervals for his young Indian friend.

It was night. No accident had occurred beyond the laceration of two of Ephraim Giles's fingers, who having that day been presented with a new suit by the doctor--the fac-simile in fashion of the old--had been whittling almost in front of one of the guns when discharged, and lost, with the skin of his finger, both his stick and his knife. The sultriness of the day had been succeeded by a cool and refreshing air. Gaiety and content every where prevailed, and many were the voices--male and female--that exclaimed, as allusion was made to the ceremony all knew, to be in progress: "God bless them, and make them happy, as they deserve to be." A large tub of whisky-punch, the gift of the commanding officer, had been brewed by Von Vottenberg, for their mid-day revel, and this, all had been unanimous in pronouncing the best medicine the doctor had ever administered to them; and now in small social messes, seated round their rude tables, covered with tin goblets, and pitchers of the same metal--the mothers with their children at their side or upon their knees, and the fathers and unmarried men puffing clouds of smoke from their short pipes--which they filled from two others placed on an elevated settle--one in each block house --which the happy Ronayne had given them on the occasion.

Even the guard was moderately supplied, and the sentries alone, pacing to and fro in their limited walk, felt the bitterness of privation, as they counted the minutes that must elapse before they could join in the festivities which the loud voice and ringing laugh, occasionally wafted to their ears, told them were in progress.

In the rooms of the commanding officer there was more than the usual manifestation of the anniversary. All had dined at an early hour, but a large side-board that stood in one corner of the council room--always fitted up on these occasions--was covered with vases containing wines, liqueurs, juleps, and punches of various kinds--the latter the work of the indefatigable son of Esculapius, and of these the host and his guests partook freely, in commemoration of the day. At the opposite end of the room had been raised a sort of tribune for the orator of the day, but as it was intended the address should be impromptu, no name had been mentioned, nor could any one know, until the moment when the majority of voices should select him on whom the office was to devolve. In the fear entertained by each that he should be the party selected, the glass, to impart the necessary courage, was not spared. But he who was not in the room, or of the number of those devoted to the punch-bowl was the person chosen. As if by one impulsive consent, Ronayne, who was seated in the inner room, and discoursing of any thing but politics to his betrothed, found himself loudly called upon--knew it was in vain to object--and reluctantly rose in obedience to the summons.

"Come young gentleman," said Captain Headley, entering with an air of gaiety by no means usual to him, "you are, it appears, in all things," and he bowed significantly to Maria Heywood, "the chosen of the evening--but recollect," he added, as he drew his arm through his own, and proceeded towards the larger apartment where Ronayne was awaited, "as you acquit yourself of YOUR duty, so shall I of MINE."

"I shall do my best, sir," replied the youth, in the same light tone, "but of the two orations, I know which will be the best suited to my own taste."

The other ladies, with the exception of Mrs. Heywood, had also risen, and now stood grouped near Captain Headley, who, with Maria Heywood on his arm, leaned against the door-way separating the two rooms--while Ronayne, amid cheers and congratulations, made his way to the tribune, at the farther end of the apartment.

His address was necessarily not long--for independently of the impatience he could not but entertain at that moment of all subjects but that nearest his heart, he was by no means ambitious of making a display of his powers of elocution. Yet, notwithstanding this, he treated his theme in so masterly a manner, and in such perfectly good taste, omitting all expressions of that rancor towards Great Britain, which forms so leading a feature in American orations on this occasion, and yet reflecting honor on the land of his birth--alluding, moreover, to the high position even then occupied by the nation, and the future greatness which he predicted, from its laws, its institutions, and peculiar form of government, awaited it--that Maria Heywood could not fail to experience a secret pride in the warm, and evidently sincere acclamation of the little party present, attesting as they did, their estimate of the worth of him, who in another hour, would be her own for life.

As Ronayne descending from the tribune, passed to the other side of the room, he looked out of the door which had been left open, not more on account of the heat, than to afford the men and their families an opportunity of hearing the discourse thus delivered--almost the first person who came under his glance was Waunangee, for whose admission he had given orders to the serjeant of the guard, and who now, in compliance with his pressing entreaty, had attended. He was becomingly dressed in deer skin, richly embroidered, pliant and of a clear brown that harmonized well with the snowy whiteness of his linen shirt, which was fastened with silver brooches, while on the equally decorated leggins, he wore around the ankle, strings of minute brass bells. On his head floated the rich plumage of various rare birds, but no paint was visible beyond the slightest tint of vermilion on the very top of each cheek-bone, rendering even more striking the expression of his soft dark eyes.

Beckoning to him, Ronayne drew the young Indian within the door, which had he not accidentally distinguished him in the crowd, he was quite too modest to enter alone. Then drawing his arm through his own, he led him, coloring and embarrassed at the novelty of the scene, to the place where Captain Headley was still lingering with his charge. The moment they were near enough, the latter held out her hand to Waunangee, and with all the warmth of her generous nature, pressed that which he extended. The young Indian colored more deeply even than before--his hand trembled in hers--and the look of thankfulness which he bent upon her, in return for this unmistakable confidence, had all the touching melancholy of expression which she had remarked in them at their first meeting. Again a mingled sentiment of confusion and distrust suffused the cheek, and for a moment oppressed the spirit of Maria Heywood in despite of herself, and she almost wished

Waunangee had not returned. The thought however, was momentary. She felt the folly, the injustice of her feelings, and anxious to atone for them, she nervously --almost convulsively grasped the hand of the Indian, carried it to her lips, and said in her full, sweet and earnest tones, that he must ever be her brother as she would ever be his sister.

"And now," said Captain Headley to the young officer, "what reward do you expect for your maiden oration? What shall it be, Miss Heywood?"

"I will spare her the trouble of an answer," interposed Ronayne, as he took the arm which had just disengaged itself from that of the commandant, and placed it within his own, "until you have set your seal to the priceless gift," and his eyes looked all the intensity of his feeling; "I part not with it again."

"Every thing is ready is the next room," answered Captain Headley--"go in. When I have announced that the ceremony is about to take place, I shall hasten to give you the dear girl for life," and imprinting a kiss upon her brow, he passed on to those who were paying their homage to the punch-bowl, and discussing the merits of the oration just delivered.

It was with a flushed cheek, and a beating heart that Maria Heywood was led by Ronayne, radiant with hope and joy, to the little table covered with plain, white linen, and illuminated by half a dozen tall candles, behind which the commanding officer had placed himself on an elevated estrade.

All of the guests were grouped around, a little in the rear, while Lieutenant Elmsley stood on the right hand of his friend, and his wife on the left of the betrothed. Next to her, in an arm chair, which, provided with rollers, was easily moved, Mrs. Heywood--and with her beautiful arms reposing on the high back of this, stood Mrs. Headley in graceful attitude, watching the ceremony with almost maternal interest. Immediately behind Ronayne, from whom he evidently did not like to be separated, stood Waunangee, with an air of deep dejection, yet casting glances rapidly from one to the other of his two friends.

When the young officer, after having formally received the bride from her mother, whose strength barely permitted her to rise and go through that part of the ceremony, proceeded to place the ring upon the finger of his wife, it fell, either from nervousness or accident upon the matted floor. Quick as thought, Waunangee, who had now his whole attention bent upon the passing scene, stooped, picked it up, and attempted to place it on the finger, still extended, for which it was designed.

"Gently, Waunangee, my good fellow," said the officer, piqued not less at his own awkwardness at such a moment, than at the outre act of the youth, from whom he rather unceremoniously took it--"the husband only does this."

"Wah!" involuntarily exclaimed the other, his cheek becoming brighter, and his eyes kindling into sudden fierceness, while his hand intuitively clutched the handle of his knife--yet the moment afterwards relinquished it. The motion had been so quick, indeed, that only Mr. Headley and the bride herself had noticed it.

Still fascinated as it were by the novel scene, Waunangee moved not away, but the expression of his eyes had wholly changed. There was no longer to be remarked there the great melancholy of the past--but the wild restless, flashing glance that told of strong excitement within.

When immediately afterwards they knelt, and had their hands joined by Captain Headley, Waunangee bent eagerly forward, as if apprehensive of losing the slightest part of the ceremonial, but when at the conclusion, Ronayne saluted his wife in the usual manner, his cheek became suddenly pale as its native hue would permit, and with folded arms and proud attitude he withdrew slowly from the place he had hitherto occupied, to mingle more with the crowd behind.

When Ronayne, who, remembering the little incident of the ring, and the possible pique Waunangee might feel, turned to look for him, that he might again present his bride in her new character, he was no where to be seen, nor was he ever again beheld within the precincts of that stockade.

And under those singular and somewhat ominous circumstances, were the long-delayed nuptials of Harry Ronayne and Maria Heywood--the great favorites of the garrison--celebrated to the joy of all within the Fort of Chicago.

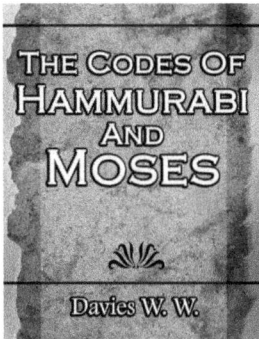

The Codes Of Hammurabi And Moses
W. W. Davies

QTY

The discovery of the Hammurabi Code is one of the greatest achievements of archaeology, and is of paramount interest, not only to the student of the Bible, but also to all those interested in ancient history...

Religion   ISBN: *1-59462-338-4*   **Pages:132**

MSRP $12.95

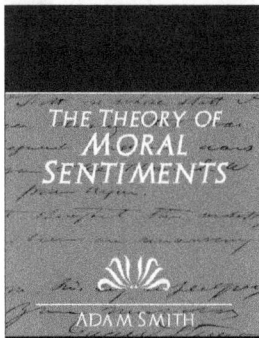

The Theory of Moral Sentiments
Adam Smith

QTY

This work from 1749. contains original theories of conscience amd moral judgment and it is the foundation for systemof morals.

Philosophy ISBN: *1-59462-777-0*   **Pages:536**

MSRP $19.95

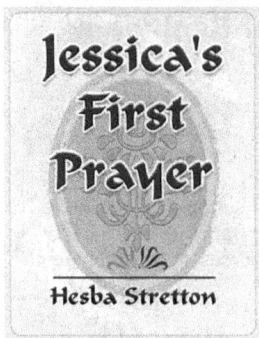

Jessica's First Prayer
Hesba Stretton

QTY

In a screened and secluded corner of one of the many railway-bridges which span the streets of London there could be seen a few years ago, from five o'clock every morning until half past eight, a tidily set-out coffee-stall, consisting of a trestle and board, upon which stood two large tin cans, with a small fire of charcoal burning under each so as to keep the coffee boiling during the early hours of the morning when the work-people were thronging into the city on their way to their daily toil...

Pages:84

Childrens   ISBN: *1-59462-373-2*   *MSRP $9.95*

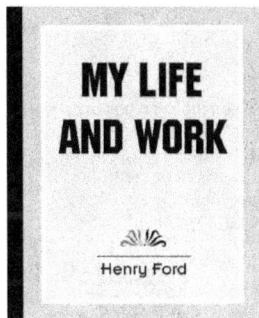

My Life and Work
Henry Ford

QTY

Henry Ford revolutionized the world with his implementation of mass production for the Model T automobile. Gain valuable business insight into his life and work with his own auto-biography... "We have only started on our development of our country we have not as yet, with all our talk of wonderful progress, done more than scratch the surface. The progress has been wonderful enough but..."

Pages:300

Biographies/   ISBN: *1-59462-198-5*   *MSRP $21.95*

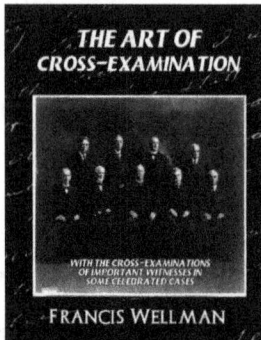

The Art of Cross-Examination
Francis Wellman

QTY

I presume it is the experience of every author, after his first book is published upon an important subject, to be almost overwhelmed with a wealth of ideas and illustrations which could readily have been included in his book, and which to his own mind, at least, seem to make a second edition inevitable. Such certainly was the case with me; and when the first edition had reached its sixth impression in five months, I rejoiced to learn that it seemed to my publishers that the book had met with a sufficiently favorable reception to justify a second and considerably enlarged edition. ..

Pages:412

Reference ISBN: *1-59462-647-2* *MSRP $19.95*

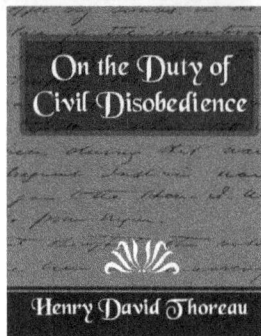

On the Duty of Civil Disobedience
Henry David Thoreau

QTY

Thoreau wrote his famous essay, On the Duty of Civil Disobedience, as a protest against an unjust but popular war and the immoral but popular institution of slave-owning. He did more than write—he declined to pay his taxes, and was hauled off to gaol in consequence. Who can say how much this refusal of his hastened the end of the war and of slavery ?

Law ISBN: *1-59462-747-9* **Pages:48**

MSRP $7.45

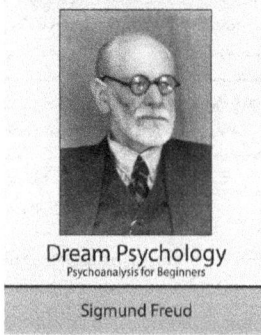

Dream Psychology Psychoanalysis for Beginners
Sigmund Freud

QTY

Sigmund Freud, born Sigismund Schlomo Freud (May 6, 1856 - September 23, 1939), was a Jewish-Austrian neurologist and psychiatrist who co-founded the psychoanalytic school of psychology. Freud is best known for his theories of the unconscious mind, especially involving the mechanism of repression; his redefinition of sexual desire as mobile and directed towards a wide variety of objects; and his therapeutic techniques, especially his understanding of transference in the therapeutic relationship and the presumed value of dreams as sources of insight into unconscious desires.

Pages:196

Psychology ISBN: *1-59462-905-6* *MSRP $15.45*

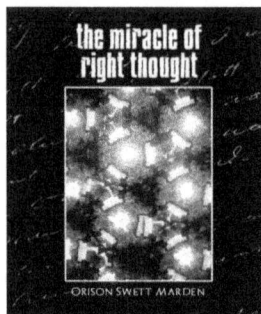

The Miracle of Right Thought
Orison Swett Marden

QTY

Believe with all of your heart that you will do what you were made to do. When the mind has once formed the habit of holding cheerful, happy, prosperous pictures, it will not be easy to form the opposite habit. It does not matter how improbable or how far away this realization may see, or how dark the prospects may be, if we visualize them as best we can, as vividly as possible, hold tenaciously to them and vigorously struggle to attain them, they will gradually become actualized, realized in the life. But a desire, a longing without endeavor, a yearning abandoned or held indifferently will vanish without realization.

Pages:360

Self Help ISBN: *1-59462-644-8* *MSRP $25.45*

The Rosicrucian Cosmo-Conception Mystic Christianity by *Max Heindel*   ISBN: *1-59462-188-8*   **$38.95**
The Rosicrucian Cosmo-conception is not dogmatic, neither does it appeal to any other authority than the reason of the student. It is: not controversial, but is: sent forth in the, hope that it may help to clear...   *New Age/Religion Pages 646*

Abandonment To Divine Providence by *Jean-Pierre de Caussade*   ISBN: *1-59462-228-0*   **$25.95**
"The Rev. Jean Pierre de Caussade was one of the most remarkable spiritual writers of the Society of Jesus in France in the 18th Century. His death took place at Toulouse in 1751. His works have gone through many editions and have been republished...   *Inspirational/Religion Pages 400*

Mental Chemistry by *Charles Haanel*   ISBN: *1-59462-192-6*   **$23.95**
Mental Chemistry allows the change of material conditions by combining and appropriately utilizing the power of the mind. Much like applied chemistry creates something new and unique out of careful combinations of chemicals the mastery of mental chemistry...   *New Age Pages 354*

The Letters of Robert Browning and Elizabeth Barret Barrett 1845-1846 vol II   ISBN: *1-59462-193-4*   **$35.95**
by *Robert Browning* and *Elizabeth Barrett*   *Biographies Pages 596*

Gleanings In Genesis (volume I) by *Arthur W. Pink*   ISBN: *1-59462-001-6*   **$27.45**
Appropriately has Genesis been termed "the seed plot of the Bible" for in it we have, in germ form, almost all of the great doctrines which are afterwards fully developed in the books of Scripture which follow...   *Religion/Inspirational Pages 420*

The Master Key by *L. W. de Laurence*   ISBN: *1-59462-001-6*   **$30.95**
In no branch of human knowledge has there been a more lively increase of the spirit of research during the past few years than in the study of Psychology, Concentration and Mental Discipline. The requests for authentic lessons in Thought Control, Mental Discipline and...   *New Age/Business Pages 422*

The Lesser Key Of Solomon Goetia by *L. W. de Laurence*   ISBN: *1-59462-092-X*   **$9.95**
This translation of the first book of the "Lernegton" which is now for the first time made accessible to students of Talismanic Magic was done, after careful collation and edition, from numerous Ancient Manuscripts in Hebrew, Latin, and French...   *New Age/Occult Pages 92*

Rubaiyat Of Omar Khayyam by *Edward Fitzgerald*   ISBN:*1-59462-332-5*   **$13.95**
Edward Fitzgerald, whom the world has already learned, in spite of his own efforts to remain within the shadow of anonymity, to look upon as one of the rarest poets of the century, was born at Bredfield, in Suffolk, on the 31st of March, 1809. He was the third son of John Purcell...   *Music Pages 172*

Ancient Law by *Henry Maine*   ISBN: *1-59462-128-4*   **$29.95**
The chief object of the following pages is to indicate some of the earliest ideas of mankind, as they are reflected in Ancient Law, and to point out the relation of those ideas to modern thought.   *Religion/History Pages 452*

Far-Away Stories by *William J. Locke*   ISBN: *1-59462-129-2*   **$19.45**
"Good wine needs no bush,' but a collection of mixed vintages does. And this book is just such a collection. Some of the stories I do not want to remain buried for ever in the museum files of dead magazine-numbers an author's not unpardonable vanity..."   *Fiction Pages 272*

Life of David Crockett by *David Crockett*   ISBN: *1-59462-250-7*   **$27.45**
"Colonel David Crockett was one of the most remarkable men of the times in which he lived. Born in humble life, but gifted with a strong will, an indomitable courage, and unremitting perseverance...   *Biographies/New Age Pages 424*

Lip-Reading by *Edward Nitchie*   ISBN: *1-59462-206-X*   **$25.95**
Edward B. Nitchie, founder of the New York School for the Hard of Hearing, now the Nitchie School of Lip-Reading, Inc, wrote "LIP-READING Principles and Practice". The development and perfecting of this meritorious work on lip-reading was an undertaking...   *How-to Pages 400*

A Handbook of Suggestive Therapeutics, Applied Hypnotism, Psychic Science   ISBN: *1-59462-214-0*   **$24.95**
by *Henry Munro*   *Health/New Age/Health/Self-help Pages 376*

A Doll's House: and Two Other Plays by *Henrik Ibsen*   ISBN: *1-59462-112-8*   **$19.95**
Henrik Ibsen created this classic when in revolutionary 1848 Rome. Introducing some striking concepts in playwriting for the realist genre, this play has been studied the world over.   *Fiction/Classics/Plays 308*

The Light of Asia by *sir Edwin Arnold*   ISBN: *1-59462-204-3*   **$13.95**
In this poetic masterpiece, Edwin Arnold describes the life and teachings of Buddha. The man who was to become known as Buddha to the world was born as Prince Gautama of India but he rejected the worldly riches and abandoned the reigns of power when... Religion/History/Biographies Pages 170

The Complete Works of Guy de Maupassant by *Guy de Maupassant*   ISBN: *1-59462-157-8*   **$16.95**
"For days and days, nights and nights, I had dreamed of that first kiss which was to consecrate our engagement, and I knew not on what spot I should put my lips..."   *Fiction/Classics Pages 240*

The Art of Cross-Examination by *Francis L. Wellman*   ISBN: *1-59462-309-0*   **$26.95**
Written by a renowned trial lawyer, Wellman imparts his experience and uses case studies to explain how to use psychology to extract desired information through questioning.   *How-to/Science/Reference Pages 408*

Answered or Unanswered? by *Louisa Vaughan*   ISBN: *1-59462-248-5*   **$10.95**
Miracles of Faith in China   *Religion Pages 112*

The Edinburgh Lectures on Mental Science (1909) by *Thomas*   ISBN: *1-59462-008-3*   **$11.95**
This book contains the substance of a course of lectures recently given by the writer in the Queen Street Hall, Edinburgh. Its purpose is to indicate the Natural Principles governing the relation between Mental Action and Material Conditions...   *New Age/Psychology Pages 148*

Ayesha by *H. Rider Haggard*   ISBN: *1-59462-301-5*   **$24.95**
Verily and indeed it is the unexpected that happens! Probably if there was one person upon the earth from whom the Editor of this, and of a certain previous history, did not expect to hear again...   *Classics Pages 380*

Ayala's Angel by *Anthony Trollope*   ISBN: *1-59462-352-X*   **$29.95**
The two girls were both pretty, but Lucy who was twenty-one who supposed to be simple and comparatively unattractive, whereas Ayala was credited, as her Bombwhat romantic name might show, with poetic charm and a taste for romance. Ayala when her father died was nineteen... Fiction Pages 484

The American Commonwealth by *James Bryce*   ISBN: *1-59462-286-8*   **$34.45**
An interpretation of American democratic political theory. It examines political mechanics and society from the perspective of Scotsman James Bryce   *Politics Pages 572*

Stories of the Pilgrims by *Margaret P. Pumphrey*   ISBN: *1-59462-116-2*   **$17.95**
This book explores pilgrims religious oppression in England as well as their escape to Holland and eventual crossing to America on the Mayflower, and their early days in New England...   *History Pages 268*

QTY

The Fasting Cure *by Sinclair Upton*   ISBN: *1-59462-222-1*   **$13.95**

In the Cosmopolitan Magazine for May, 1910, and in the Contemporary Review (London) for April, 1910, I published an article dealing with my experiences in fasting. I have written a great many magazine articles, but never one which attracted so much attention...   New Age/Self Help/Health Pages 164

Hebrew Astrology *by Sepharial*   ISBN: *1-59462-308-2*   **$13.45**

In these days of advanced thinking it is a matter of common observation that we have left many of the old landmarks behind and that we are now pressing forward to greater heights and to a wider horizon than that which represented the mind-content of our progenitors...   Astrology Pages 144

Thought Vibration or The Law of Attraction in the Thought World   ISBN: *1-59462-127-6*   **$12.95**

by William Walker Atkinson   Psychology/Religion Pages 144

Optimism *by Helen Keller*   ISBN: *1-59462-108-X*   **$15.95**

Helen Keller was blind, deaf, and mute since 19 months old, yet famously learned how to overcome these handicaps, communicate with the world, and spread her lectures promoting optimism. An inspiring read for everyone...   Biographies/Inspirational Pages 84

Sara Crewe *by Frances Burnett*   ISBN: *1-59462-360-0*   **$9.45**

In the first place, Miss Minchin lived in London. Her home was a large, dull, tall one, in a large, dull square, where all the houses were alike, and all the sparrows were alike, and where all the door-knockers made the same heavy sound...   Childrens/Classic Pages 88

The Autobiography of Benjamin Franklin *by Benjamin Franklin*   ISBN: *1-59462-135-7*   **$24.95**

The Autobiography of Benjamin Franklin has probably been more extensively read than any other American historical work, and no other book of its kind has had such ups and downs of fortune. Franklin lived for many years in England, where he was agent...   Biographies/History Pages 332

Name	
Email	
Telephone	
Address	
City, State ZIP	

☐ **Credit Card**   ☐ **Check / Money Order**

Credit Card Number	
Expiration Date	
Signature	

Please Mail to: Book Jungle
PO Box 2226
Champaign, IL 61825
or Fax to: 630-214-0564

ORDERING INFORMATION

web*: www.bookjungle.com*
email*: sales@bookjungle.com*
fax*: 630-214-0564*
mail*: Book Jungle PO Box 2226 Champaign, IL 61825*
or PayPal *to sales@bookjungle.com*

Please contact us for bulk discounts

DIRECT-ORDER TERMS

**20% Discount if You Order
Two or More Books**
Free Domestic Shipping!
Accepted: Master Card, Visa,
Discover, American Express

www.ingramcontent.com/pod-product-compliance
Lightning Source LLC
Chambersburg PA
CBHW080532090426
42733CB00015B/2562